Colorado Legends, Myths, and More

Amanda Blackwood

MANDOLIN PUBLISHING

Published by the Mandolin Publishing Group

Now, let's get real: most events have been compressed, like a suitcase packed for a week-long vacation in under five minutes. Any randomly italicized words you see are simply for the dramatic effect; they do not indicate that the author is whispering sweet nothings.

This book's content is as up-to-date as a cat meme from August 2024, based on all the information the author managed to scrape together from the vast world of the internet (and maybe a few local gossip sessions).

What Makes Something a Legend or Myth?

Legends and myths have woven themselves into the fabric of human storytelling, enchanting listeners and readers for centuries. But what exactly makes a tale a legend or a myth, and why do we cling to these narratives with the same fervor we reserve for our favorite snacks during movie night? At their core, both legends and myths are stories that transcend time, providing us with explanations for the inexplicable, morals for the muddled, and sometimes just a good laugh at humanity's expense.

A legend is often rooted in historical events or figures, albeit embellished to the point where you might wonder if the storyteller had one too many cups of coffee. Take, for example, the tale of King Arthur and the Knights of the Round Table. While Arthur may have been based on a real leader, the addition of magical swords, mystical islands, and talking animals transforms him into a figure that seems more suited for a theme park than a history book. Legends typically involve larger-than-life characters who face monumental challenges, making us wonder how they manage to keep their capes so wrinkle-free amidst all that drama.

Myths, on the other hand, dive deeper into the realm of the divine and the supernatural. These stories often seek to explain natural phenomena or the human condition through the antics of gods, demigods, and fantastical creatures. Take Zeus, for instance. The king of the Greek gods was known for his lightning bolts and questionable romantic choices. Myths like these serve a dual purpose: they provide entertainment and offer explanations for why things happen the way they do, like why the sun rises in the east or why our socks disappear in the laundry—thank you, mischievous laundry gods!

Both legends and myths often emerge from cultural contexts, reflecting the values, fears, and aspirations of the societies that create them. They act as mirrors, allowing us to see ourselves in the stories we tell. The hero's journey, a common theme in both legends and myths, speaks to our universal desire for growth, adventure, and occasionally, the chance to rescue a damsel or dragon in distress. However, let's not forget that sometimes the real hero is the one who shows up with pizza during a late-night storytelling session.

Humor plays a crucial role in the longevity of these tales. After all, who doesn't love a good chuckle while navigating the complexities of existence? Many legends and myths contain elements of absurdity that make them memorable. Consider the tale of the Trojan Horse, where an entire city fell for a gift that was essentially a massive wooden piñata filled with sneaky soldiers. It's as if the Greeks said, "Hey, let's try this trick! What could possibly go wrong?" This blend of intrigue and hilarity keeps these stories alive, allowing them to be retold and reimagined across generations.

Additionally, the embellishment of these stories contributes to their legendary status. Over time, details are added, altered, or simply exaggerated until you're left with a tale so far removed from reality that it resembles a game of telephone gone wildly off course. One can only imagine the original version of the story of Paul Bunyan, where he started as a humble lumberjack, but by the time it reaches the final telling, he's wrestling bears while simultaneously creating the Grand Canyon with a single swing of his axe. Now that's a lumberjack with some serious multitasking skills!

Cultural exchange also plays a significant role in the creation of legends and myths. As stories traverse borders, they are adapted to fit new audiences and contexts, leading to the creation of hybrids that reflect a rich tapestry of influences. Consider how the story of Robin Hood has morphed over the centuries, shifting from a simple outlaw tale to a swashbuckling hero in tights who steals from the rich and gives to the poor, all while dodging arrows and serenading Maid Marian.

At their core, legends and myths resonate because they capture something essential about the human experience. They address our fears, aspirations, and the curious question of why we find ourselves knee-deep in chaos more often than not. They remind us that even in the face of adversity, laughter can be a powerful tool. After all, if a legend can transform a simple man into a mighty warrior or a myth can make an all-powerful god fall in love with a mortal, then surely we can face our own challenges with a wink and a nod.

The myths and legends of Colorado have a unique ability to endure through the ages, captivating the imaginations of locals and visitors alike. At first glance, these tales might seem like whimsical stories spun from the mountains and plains of this rugged state, but they serve a far deeper purpose. The enduring nature of these myths and legends can be attributed to a blend of Colorado's rich history, the striking landscapes that shape its narratives, and the fundamental human desire for connection, understanding, and a good story.

One of the key elements contributing to the longevity of Colorado's myths and legends is the state's fascinating history. From the indigenous peoples who first inhabited the land to the waves of settlers who arrived during the Gold Rush, Colorado's past is rife with dramatic events and larger-than-life characters. These historical narratives often become the foundation for myths, as they are transformed over time into tales that reflect not only the events but also the cultural values and fears of the people who tell them. Take the legend of the "Lost Dutchman Mine," for example. This tale, which speaks of hidden gold in the mountains, resonates with the dreams of wealth and discovery that defined the spirit of the pioneers. While its roots may lie in historical encounters and expeditions, the allure of treasure and adventure keeps the legend alive, sparking the imagination of those who hear it.

Moreover, Colorado's stunning natural landscapes play a significant role in the endurance of its myths. The state's majestic mountains, deep canyons, and vast plains are not just backdrops but characters in their own right. These geographical features often inspire legends that personify the land, weaving narratives around them that reflect their beauty, danger, and mystery. For instance, the story of the "Bunny Man," a supposed spectral figure that haunts the backwoods of the state, utilizes the dark and enchanting nature of Colorado's forests to create an atmosphere of intrigue and fear. The landscape itself becomes a living part of the story, enhancing the legend and inviting those curious enough to seek out its truth.

Additionally, the human desire for connection and understanding plays a vital role in why these myths and legends endure. Stories have always been a way for people to connect with one another, to share experiences, and to explore the unknown. In Colorado, legends often serve as a bridge between generations, with grandparents sharing tales of mountain ghosts or ancient spirits with their grandchildren around a crackling campfire. These stories not only entertain but also impart valuable lessons about courage, perseverance, and the complexities of life. In this sense, the act of storytelling becomes a communal experience, fostering a sense of belonging and shared identity that reinforces the importance of these myths.

Cultural diversity also enriches Colorado's mythological tapestry. The state has a unique blend of indigenous narratives, settler folklore, and modern interpretations that come together to create a vibrant storytelling landscape. The tales of Native American tribes, such as the Ute, Arapaho, and Cheyenne, provide deep-rooted legends that speak to their connection with the land, the spirits, and their historical experiences. When these stories mingle with those of early European settlers and contemporary residents, a dynamic cultural exchange occurs, giving rise to new myths that reflect the evolving identity of Colorado. This intermingling of narratives keeps the legends fresh and relevant, allowing them to adapt to changing societal values and challenges.

Furthermore, the accessibility of Colorado's legends and myths plays a crucial role in their longevity. In an age where information can be easily disseminated, these stories often find new life through various mediums. Books, documentaries, local folklore festivals, and even social media platforms allow people to share and engage with these narratives in innovative ways. A story that may have been whispered in the shadows of a mountain cabin can now reach a global audience, captivating hearts and sparking curiosity far beyond Colorado's borders. The ease with which people can access and share these legends contributes to their resilience and adaptability over time.

Finally, humor often threads its way through Colorado's myths, lending a lighthearted touch that helps them endure. Whether it's a tall tale about a drunken prospector or a quirky ghost story involving a mischievous mountain spirit, these narratives provide laughter and entertainment, making them more memorable and enjoyable. When stories have a sprinkle of humor, they become a part of social gatherings, passed along with a chuckle or a wink. This comedic element ensures that the legends remain vibrant and engaging, allowing them to withstand the test of time.

The enduring nature of Colorado's myths and legends can be attributed to a harmonious blend of rich history, stunning landscapes, cultural diversity, human connection, accessibility, and humor. These tales encapsulate the spirit of the state, weaving together the past and present while inviting new generations to explore, interpret, and enjoy them. As long as there are mountains to climb and campfires to gather around, the stories of Colorado will continue to be told, creating a legacy that connects people across time and space.

Ghosts of the Rockies

As the sun dipped below the jagged peaks of the Rockies, casting a golden hue over the sprawling Colorado landscape, the air grew heavy with the whispers of legends long forgotten. It was a time to gather around the flickering flames of a campfire, where the shadows danced like the spirits of those who once roamed these mountains. Tonight, we would share the stories that bound us to this land, the tales that wove together history, myth, and the inexplicable presence of the otherworldly.

The stars twinkled like a million watchful eyes, their light illuminating the stories etched in the minds of those gathered. Old-timers settled into their chairs, mugs of steaming cocoa in hand, while the younger ones listened intently, eyes wide with both wonder and a touch of trepidation. Here in Colorado, the mountains weren't just a backdrop—they were alive with history, and many claimed to have felt the brush of ghostly fingers against their skin, or heard the soft echo of voices carried by the wind.

"Let me tell you about **Silver Heels**," began a weathered miner, his voice gravelly but warm. "She was a dance hall girl in Buckskin Joe, a vision of beauty who captured the hearts of all. But when smallpox swept through the camp, she became the unlikeliest of heroes, nursing the sick until she vanished without a trace. Some say her ghost still walks the cemetery, leaving flowers at the graves of those she cared for. They say if you're lucky—or perhaps unlucky—you might catch a glimpse of her heavily veiled figure gliding through the night, her heart still heavy with the love she had for her fellow miners."

The young ones leaned closer, shivering not just from the chill of the night but from the thrill of her tale. The flickering firelight cast an otherworldly glow, as if the spirits of Silver Heels and her miners were joining in the gathering.

"Ah, but don't forget about the train ghost!" interjected another voice, the town historian, eyes sparkling with mischief. "Old Nelson Edwards was a railroad engineer who crossed **Marshall Pass** one fateful night. He felt a presence behind him, a phantom train racing to catch up. They say the train never existed, but the adrenaline was real enough! Edwards saw it tumble into the canyon, yet no wreck was ever found. Some claim that if you listen closely near the pass, you can still hear the whistle of that ghostly locomotive echoing through the valleys, chasing after those who dare to cross its path."

A collective gasp arose from the younger listeners. They had ventured into these mountains but had never stopped to consider that the echoes they heard might be something more than just the wind or the rustling of leaves.

"Then there's Molly Brown," said a third voice, a soft-spoken woman who had spent years researching the legend of the Titanic survivor. "They say her spirit still wanders the halls of her mansion in Denver, keeping a watchful eye on her beloved city. She may have survived a sinking ship, but in the end, she never left."

The stories flowed like the rivers that carved through the mountains—sometimes gentle, sometimes wild, but always leaving their mark. The tales of Alma, a town where the dead refuse to rest, blended seamlessly with the legend of Tommyknockers, the mischievous spirits believed to be the miners' guardians. Everyone knew of their playful antics, the sounds of pickaxes echoing in the night, as if the spirits were still searching for their lost gold.

As the fire crackled, the temperature dropped, and the wind picked up, causing the branches of the surrounding trees to sway and whisper, almost in agreement with the tales being told. The group huddled closer together, the heat from the flames providing a sense of safety against the shadows lurking just beyond the firelight.

"Every legend, every ghost story we've shared," the historian continued, "reminds us that we are not alone. These mountains have seen joy, sorrow, love, and loss. The spirits here are tied to the land; they are the very fabric of Colorado's history. They remind us of the bravery, the folly, and the passions that have shaped our lives."

As the night deepened and the stories continued, the atmosphere shifted, an electric charge filling the air. The campfire's glow flickered, casting long shadows that seemed to swirl and dance like the spirits themselves. Just beyond the light, a chill breeze swept through the gathering, and for a brief moment, the group fell silent, sensing an unseen presence—a reminder that the past was always close at hand.

As the final story was told, and laughter faded into a respectful silence, a single howl echoed through the mountains, resonating like a haunting chorus. The gathered souls felt a connection to those who had come before them, a shared bond with the ghosts of Colorado, both legendary and real.

"Remember," the historian said softly, his eyes twinkling in the firelight, "we are part of this story, too. The legends of Colorado will carry on through us. We may not see the spirits, but they're always here, watching over us, encouraging us to continue creating our own stories. So, the next time you find yourself in these mountains, listen closely. You might just hear a whisper in the wind, a gentle reminder that legends never truly die—they live on in the hearts of those who remember."

As the final embers glowed and the group began to pack up, a sense of camaraderie lingered in the air, blending with the echoes of the past. Each person carried with them the warmth of the stories shared, the legends that would live on long after the fire had died down, illuminating the night sky with the promise of more tales to come.

With one last glance at the moonlit peaks, they departed, leaving behind not just a campfire, but the enduring spirit of

Colorado, where myths and memories intertwine, reminding all who dare to listen that the past is never too far behind.

The Barber's Last Cut

It was the year 1884, and Leadville barber John F. Fitzgerald, like many men of the time, found himself succumbing to the allure of Denver's darker side. With his trusty razor in hand and a pocket full of bills, he told his wife a simple tale about visiting a friend in the big city. Of course, this "friend" was none other than the Mile High City's infamous Holladay Street, a place where virtuous women and honest men were about as common as snowflakes in July. Even the Rocky Mountain News, known for its somewhat restrained reporting, didn't mince words, calling it a place where decency was regarded with "vast suspicion." Translation: if you showed up in Denver looking like a saint, you were probably the biggest sinner in town.

Fitzgerald, a man of modest means and, it turns out, modest judgment, made the journey to Denver in search of a good time. But Denver in 1884 wasn't just any city—it was the Wild West in all its raw, gritty glory. The saloons were packed with gamblers, the streets with shady characters, and the brothels with... well, let's just say they weren't selling scented candles. Holladay Street, in particular, was where the fun could quickly turn fatal. And for Fitzgerald, his night of "fun" would be his last.

After a few rounds of gambling, likely fueled by cheap whiskey and bad decisions, Fitzgerald's night led him to

Belle Worden's house of ill repute, where he caught the attention of not just the ladies, but also a nefarious crew led by Belle herself. And what did Fitzgerald do that sealed his fate? He flashed a respectable roll of cash. A move that, on these streets, was like waving a slab of raw meat in front of a starving pack of wolves.

As the story goes, Fitzgerald was lured upstairs by Mattie Lemon, one of Belle's more... persuasive employees. After what can only be described as an evening of "rest," Fitzgerald drifted off to sleep. It was then that Belle, Mattie, and a man named Berry Gates—who was, according to the Rocky Mountain News, Mattie's "handyman, hatchetman, and spare-time lover" (talk about a résumé)—made their move. Gates "expertly" slit Fitzgerald's throat, and the women held him down, all while being careful not to ruin their clothes. Because in the business of murder, the last thing you want is to look like you've been caught red-handed. Literally.

For their trouble, they walked away with a grand total of $115 and a gold watch. Not quite the jackpot they were hoping for, but it was enough to make them feel like they'd pulled off a master crime. That is, until Fitzgerald's body was found two months later, floating in Cherry Creek like the world's worst time capsule.

It was three young boys playing by the creek who first saw his hand sticking out of the mud—an unpleasant surprise to say the least. By the time the authorities arrived, a crowd of

1,000 onlookers had gathered to watch as a crew of men, armed with spades, dug out the barber's decomposing body. "The body was badly decomposed, and it was almost impossible to remove the clothing," reported the Rocky Mountain News, ever helpful in painting a charming picture. But amidst the decay, one thing stood out: Fitzgerald's barber tools, still intact, and inscribed with his name. It was all the proof they needed—John F. Fitzgerald had gambled his life away, and lost in more ways than one.

The investigation didn't take long. Neighbors recalled hearing cries of "Murder!" coming from Belle Worden's house on the fateful night Fitzgerald was last seen. Of course, in a place like Holladay Street, cries of murder were about as common as the clinking of poker chips. "There were similar cries almost every night," the newspaper noted, "and they didn't really mean anything." But this time, they did.

Within days, police arrested Belle, Mattie, Gates, and a man named Charles Smith, who had helpfully confessed on behalf of the group. The trial that followed was a spectacle, with each of the accused pleading innocence despite overwhelming evidence to the contrary. And yet, when the jury returned with a guilty verdict, the judge showed them an inexplicable kindness, sentencing each to only 10 years in prison. Talk about a light sentence for a heavy crime.

As the convicted murderers left the courthouse, they could be heard chatting about what jobs they might want during their prison stint, as if they were headed to a summer camp instead of the penitentiary. And Fitzgerald? His ghost is said to haunt Union Station, the very place where he began his ill-fated journey to Denver's underworld. Locals swear that on quiet nights, you can still hear the faint sound of a straight razor scraping across stubble, followed by a whisper on the wind: "Don't forget to tip your barber."

Denver in 1884 wasn't a place for the faint of heart, and John F. Fitzgerald learned that the hard way. He came looking for a good time, but what he found was a cautionary tale—a tale of greed, betrayal, and bad company. And as for the rest of us? Well, we're just lucky enough to be reading about it and not living it.

Spirits and Slots at Colorado Grande

Nestled in the heart of Central City, Colorado, where the air is thin and the stories are thicker than a ghost's sheet, stands the Colorado Grande Casino and Hotel. But before it was a place for high-stakes gambling and dubious buffet selections, the building housed the Fairley Bros. & Lampman drugstore, a barbershop, and professional offices—because nothing says "fine living" quite like getting a haircut and a prescription refill under the same roof. Built in 1896, this three-story structure has seen the rise and fall of fortunes, witnessed bloody mining strikes, and kept quiet during some rather scandalous town gossip that even today would make your grandma blush.

The Colorado Grande isn't just famous for its gambling; it proudly lays claim to the title of one of the most haunted locations in the United States. Now, you might think that the only spirits found in a casino are the ones that come in bottles, but I assure you, this place has a different kind of nightlife—one that involves ethereal figures, spooky whispers, and a sprinkle of good old-fashioned Irish charm.

Among the many tales of the supernatural, the most famous ghost is a delightful apparition known as Maggie. Picture her:

a beautiful young woman with flowing red hair, roaming the halls of the casino with an upbeat demeanor that could put even the grumpiest poker player in a good mood. Maggie is said to hang around the second and third floors, presumably avoiding the gambling tables, though local lore has it that she enjoys "trying her luck" at the slots. This is especially curious considering the casino didn't even install slot machines until 1991. Talk about a spirit with a keen sense of foresight—or perhaps a touch of existential confusion!

Legend has it that Maggie is often spotted with a male spirit, though who he is remains a mystery. Some speculate he could be a former boyfriend or a hapless coworker, which raises an important question: Is this the afterlife equivalent of a "meet-cute"? We can only imagine their spirited conversations about the latest in ghostly fashion trends or the best techniques for slipping through walls unnoticed.

As if that weren't enough, Maggie has a habit of serenading the lonely halls at night, giving late-night security guards a fright that would make even the most seasoned ghostbuster double-check their coffee intake. Just when you think you're alone, a sweet melody floats through the air, and when the guards muster the courage to investigate, she vanishes quicker than a losing bet. Now that's some serious commitment to a dramatic exit!

But wait—there's more! The casino is also home to a pint-sized specter named Lily. This little ghost has a particular affinity for purple balloons, and she doesn't take kindly to other colors. Employees have learned this lesson the hard way: leave a balloon of any shade other than purple, and it'll pop faster than you can say "paranormal activity." However, if you leave Lily a purple balloon, it floats around like a mischievous child, dancing through the air as if possessed by an otherworldly spirit (which, you know, she technically is). It seems Lily has a knack for keeping the casino lively, proving that even in the afterlife, you can still have a good time—and a good giggle.

As the sun sets and the neon lights of the casino flicker to life, visitors often find themselves enveloped in a strange blend of excitement and eeriness. For those hoping to catch a glimpse of Maggie or witness Lily's balloon antics, the Colorado Grande offers a unique blend of history, hauntings, and the occasional jackpot. After all, who wouldn't want to gamble alongside a friendly ghost or two?

So, the next time you find yourself at the Colorado Grande Casino and Hotel, keep your eyes peeled and your balloons purple. Who knows? You might just make a few ghostly friends along the way. And remember, if you hear someone singing a sweet Irish tune or see a glowing orb dancing around, it's probably not just the whiskey talking. You may have just stumbled into a lively after-hours gathering of the resident spirits—one where the chips are always stacked in their favor!

The Penitentes: A Brotherhood of the Bold and the Bonkers

In the rugged foothills of the Rocky Mountains, where the sagebrush sways like it's doing the cha-cha and the sun shines brighter than a kid's grin on a snow day, lies a lesser-known gem of American history: the Brotherhood of the Penitente. Now, if you've never heard of them, don't worry—you're not alone. It's a little surprising, considering that they had a penchant for dramatic flair that could put even the most overzealous reality TV stars to shame.

Picture this: it's the late 18th century, and Spanish settlers are trying to make a life for themselves in the American Southwest. Enter the Penitentes, a group of men who took their faith so seriously that they were willing to go to extremes. They didn't just pray in peace; they decided that the best way to demonstrate their devotion was through some good old-fashioned suffering. Forget yoga and meditation; these guys were more into self-flagellation and reenacting crucifixions. It's as if they thought, "If Jesus could hang around for hours on a cross, surely we can whip ourselves into shape!"

Now, let's clarify something right off the bat: the Penitentes weren't your run-of-the-mill churchgoers. No potluck dinners or choir practices for them. Instead, they preferred to hold clandestine meetings in secluded spots—often deep in canyons where they wouldn't be spotted by judgmental neighbors. Think of it as the ultimate "let's keep this between us" club, only instead of gossiping about the latest scandals in town, they were busy nailing each other to wooden crosses. It was the kind of brotherhood that made the Boy Scouts look like a knitting circle.

The name "Penitente," which translates to "the penitent one," was fitting given their flair for the dramatic. When it came to their rituals, the Penitentes believed that by physically punishing themselves, they could atone for their sins and the sins of the community. So, if you were feeling particularly guilty about not returning that borrowed lawnmower, you might just find yourself at a Penitente meeting, pondering whether a little self-flagellation might ease your conscience. "I swear, I'll return it next week!" you'd mumble between whips.

One of their favorite haunts was Penitente Canyon, where the steep cliffs and winding trails provided an ideal backdrop for their eccentric gatherings. The canyon was more than just a pretty face; it was a stage for their rituals. While most people would hike to enjoy the views or maybe catch a glimpse of a deer or two, the Penitentes were busy putting on their own version of a biblical drama. Rumor has it that their performances were so intense that even the local wildlife would stop and stare, probably thinking, "Who are these guys, and why do they think they're in a Passion play?"

The group was all about community and support, albeit with a side of existential dread. They'd provide help to their neighbors in need, which is pretty noble considering their usual activities. "Need someone to fix your roof? Sure, but first, let's talk about your sins." While some may have found this approach a little too intense, it did build a unique sense of camaraderie among the brothers. Just imagine the barbecues—"Hey, pass the chips, and can you also hand me that whip? I need to feel something today!"

Over the years, the Penitentes attracted a mix of curious onlookers, skeptics, and the truly devoted. They became part of the local lore, leading to whispers about their secretive practices. "Did you hear about those guys up in the canyon?" people would murmur. "I heard they're still crucifying each other up there!" That kind of word-of-mouth spread faster than a wildfire in July, and soon enough, Penitente Canyon was as well-known for its dramatic reenactments as it was for its breathtaking vistas.

As time passed, the Penitentes began to evolve, much like the rest of society. By the 20th century, they toned down the more extreme aspects of their practices. The self-flagellation and crucifixion reenactments became a little less common, possibly due to a collective realization that it might be easier to, you know, just go to therapy instead. They began focusing more on communal prayer, charity work, and, believe it or not, vibrant Easter celebrations that would make even the most dedicated bunny blush with envy.

Today, when visitors hike through Penitente Canyon, they might feel a chill in the air or a sense of something otherworldly—a whisper of the past, if you will. Whether it's the shadow of a crucified figure or just an unusually large squirrel eyeing their snacks, the canyon still carries echoes of its unique history. So next time you're out enjoying the beauty of this remarkable place, remember the brothers who took their faith to extremes. While they may have hung on wooden crosses, they also hung out as neighbors and friends, proving that even the most unconventional groups can have a heart—albeit a slightly more dramatic one.

Legend of the Yellow Honk House

Nestled in the heart of Chaffee County, Colorado, is a tiny town called Maysville, a place so small you might miss it if you blink or if you're too busy contemplating the mysteries of the universe—like why socks seem to disappear in the laundry. But if you do manage to keep your eyes peeled, you'll stumble upon a charming little gem that stands out like a canary at a black-tie event: the Yellow Honk House.

This house isn't just any old residence; it's over a century old and painted a vibrant yellow that could only be described as "sunshine on a bad hair day." Seriously, this is the kind of color that makes you feel cheery, like a good cup of coffee on a Monday morning. It's almost as if the house itself was trying to say, "Hey, look at me! I'm brightening up your day!" Now, legend has it that the original owner, Harry Miller, had a knack for bringing a smile to the faces of passersby. Rather than hiding behind the curtains like a regular homeowner, he would sit on his porch in a chair that likely had more creaks than a haunted house, waving at drivers like he was the welcoming committee for an all-time great parade.

As the story goes, drivers who happened to pass by would wave back—because, really, who could resist such a friendly fellow? It didn't take long before they began honking in response to his waves. Imagine the scene: cars rolling by, people in them looking mildly confused as they were waved at by a cheerful man in a rocking chair. Before you knew it, the sound of car horns became synonymous with Harry and his cheerful spirit. The honking became an unspoken tradition, almost a rite of passage for anyone headed up the nearby Monarch Pass. People didn't just pass by; they honked for good luck. "Good juju!" Harry would have said if he could see what his house had become. We can only imagine that somewhere in the cosmos, he was waving back, possibly with a slight grin, and definitely thinking, "You've got it, folks! Keep those horns blaring!"

Fast forward to 2016, and we meet Joe, the newest custodian of this quirky tradition. Joe wasn't just a fan of the story; he was practically its biggest cheerleader, decked out in a yellow jersey and a foam finger that read, "Honk for Harry!" He embraced the legend with open arms, welcoming honkers with the same enthusiasm that Harry had shown years ago. "No honks for bad luck!" Joe would chime in, hands on his hips like a proud dad at a Little League game. It's as if he had taken the torch from Harry and ran a victory lap around Maysville, making sure everyone knew the importance of a good, hearty honk.

But Joe's enthusiasm didn't just stop with honking; he was also on a mission to spread the joy of the Yellow Honk House far and wide. He decided to host an annual "Honk-a-thon," an event that drew people from near and far.

The festivities included honking contests, where participants would try to out-honk each other with various sounds ranging from dignified "toots" to full-blown car horn symphonies that would make Beethoven weep with envy. There were even prizes for the most creative honks, with categories like "Best Animal Impression" (which usually featured some impressive duck-like honking) and "Longest Sustained Honk" (which seemed to always end up a battle of wills between a 1992 sedan and a 2003 pickup truck).

During these events, Maysville would transform into a bustling hub of honking and laughter. Locals would set up booths selling everything from hot dogs to homemade "Honk for Good Luck" keychains, while the more ambitious residents would craft elaborate signs reading "Warning: Excessive Honking Zone!" Just imagine the tourists arriving, eyes wide with confusion, wondering if they had accidentally stumbled into a new version of a quirky state fair dedicated entirely to the art of honking.

With every honk that echoed through the valley, Joe felt a sense of pride knowing he was carrying on a legacy that had started over a hundred years ago. Drivers would approach the Yellow Honk House, some waving their arms like they were attempting to summon a flock of pigeons, while others prepared to honk with the intensity of a kid in a candy store. Joe could often be seen lounging in that same old chair Harry had once occupied, waving back at the cars like it was a high-stakes game of "who can wave the longest without breaking a smile."

And let's not forget the stories that swirled around the honking phenomenon. Rumor had it that if you honked three times while driving past the Yellow Honk House, you'd have a lucky day. There were even whispers that some daring souls had begun to honk while trying to balance a spoon on their noses—a feat that, while entirely unrelated to the honking tradition, made for some hilarious TikTok videos. "Honk while you balance!" became a phrase that echoed through the town like a battle cry for all things silly and spontaneous.

So, as the sun set over the stunning Colorado landscape, painting the mountains in hues of orange and pink, Maysville and its Yellow Honk House stood as a reminder that sometimes, a simple wave and a honk can create a connection that spans generations. And as anyone who has visited would tell you, there's no better way to kick off a road trip than by honking at a house that truly embodies the spirit of community, good luck, and a sprinkle of whimsy. After all, in a world that sometimes takes itself too seriously, a little honking never hurt anybody—unless, of course, you're honking at a cow. In that case, good luck with that!

The Legend of La Caverna del Oro

High atop the rugged terrain of Marble Mountain, Colorado, lies a tale as twisted and glittering as the veins of gold that are said to hide in its depths. Known by locals as La Caverna del Oro, or "The Cave of Gold," this limestone cave was not just a hideaway for local wildlife or a cool retreat from the blazing sun; it was once the bustling site of a gold mining operation led by Spanish adventurers who were convinced that fortune lay hidden beneath the mountain's rocky facade. They weren't just your average gold seekers either; this operation came complete with enslaved locals and even a trio of monks who seemed to think they'd stumbled onto a heavenly lottery ticket. Spoiler alert: they didn't.

The scene must have been something straight out of a Western movie, complete with the dramatic soundtrack of galloping horses and the sound of pickaxes clanging against rock. Picture this: a group of Spaniards, fueled by dreams of wealth and glory, dragging unsuspecting locals into a cave like a scene from the world's worst travel brochure. "Welcome to La Caverna del Oro! Where your hopes of riches are only matched by your chance of being forced to dig in a cave at 13,000 feet! Bring your own pickaxe!" What could possibly go wrong?

These poor souls worked tirelessly, their dreams of gold quickly overshadowed by the harsh reality of back-breaking labor and the nagging thought that their vacation to the "gold-filled paradise" had taken a darker turn. But here's the kicker—once the Spaniards had dug out what they deemed enough shiny nuggets to make their return trip to Mexico worthwhile, they decided that it would be more convenient to eliminate any witnesses. Yes, you heard that right. They killed their laborers. Apparently, nothing says "thank you for your hard work" quite like a one-way ticket to the afterlife.

Fast forward to 1869, when a man named Captain Elisha Horn decided to take his own shot at fame and fortune. With the kind of optimism only the promise of gold can provide, he claimed to have found La Caverna del Oro marked by a mysterious cross painted near the entrance, along with the remains of a Spanish soldier. Now, one has to wonder what this soldier was doing up there—perhaps he was hoping for a quiet afternoon of fishing that just happened to take a deadly turn? Whatever the case, Horn was convinced he had struck gold, quite literally, and set about drawing in a curious crowd of treasure hunters.

As word spread faster than a rumor at a high school lunch table, aspiring spelunkers from all corners of the country flocked to Marble Mountain, determined to find this elusive wooden door that supposedly concealed a treasure trove of gold. They must have envisioned themselves as modern-day conquistadors, ready to unearth riches that would make their names legendary. But alas, reality often has a way of crashing dreams like a poorly built bridge. Those who attempted to navigate the caverns quickly discovered that they were some of the most treacherous and difficult to traverse in the entire state. It's as if the cave itself was playing a cruel joke on them, whispering, "You want gold? Ha! Good luck getting to it!"

Imagine groups of would-be treasure hunters wandering through the caves, tripping over rocks and accidentally starting mini rockslides that would send them tumbling back down the mountain. The caves were filled with sharp turns, steep drops, and enough dead ends to make even the most experienced spelunker question their life choices. Some might have even wondered if they were being filmed for a reality show called "Treasure Hunters: The Most Ridiculous Adventures Ever."

Despite the odds, the allure of gold continued to draw hopeful souls into the depths of the cave. Perhaps it was the thrill of adventure, the chance to be part of a legendary story, or the faint hope that they might actually find something shiny among the darkness. They certainly had enough determination to make it a reality TV show, even if the end credits would read "Lost in the Caverns of La Caverna del Oro."

As the years rolled by, the story of La Caverna del Oro transformed from a mere tale of a gold mine into a legend filled with excitement, mystery, and a little bit of insanity. It captured the imaginations of dreamers and adventurers alike, all eager to chase the shimmering promise of gold that lay tantalizingly out of reach. And while many would leave with nothing but a few scratches and bruised egos, the cave continued to hold its secrets, deep in the heart of Marble Mountain.

Little did they know, this tale of wealth and woe was one that would go on to capture the hearts of countless adventurers, even if it turned out to be just a good yarn spun to boost newspaper sales. But for those brave enough to try and unlock the secrets of La Caverna del Oro, the journey alone was a treasure worth the trip, even if all they came away with was a good story and a healthy dose of humility. After all, in the wild world of treasure hunting, it's not just about the gold; it's about the laughter, the camaraderie, and occasionally the sheer bewilderment of wondering why you thought a cave would be a good place to spend your weekend.

The Manitou Legend of Emma Crawford

In the heart of the majestic Rocky Mountains, nestled among lush landscapes and bubbling mineral springs, lies the picturesque town of Manitou Springs, Colorado. A haven for health seekers in the late 1800s, the town was famous for its mineral-rich waters, which were believed to possess miraculous healing powers. But while some visitors were there to sip their way to wellness, others, like Emma Crawford, arrived in search of a miracle—and a wedding. Unfortunately, she found herself on a different path, one that led to the top of a mountain and, quite literally, the other side.

Emma Crawford, a spirited young woman with a heart full of hope, traveled to Manitou Springs with her mother, determined to kick tuberculosis to the curb. At the time, the disease was the leading cause of death and generally considered the uninvited guest at every social gathering. "So sorry for your loss, but at least you didn't die from the common cold!" was not the kind of consolation people offered in those days. Emma, however, was optimistic; she believed she'd soon be well enough to walk down the aisle and say, "I do," to her beloved fiancé. With visions of wedding bells and a beautiful future dancing in her head,

Emma drank her mineral water and believed she was on the mend.

But life has a funny way of taking unexpected turns, much like that one cousin who always shows up to family gatherings with a new, bewildering hairstyle. Just days before her wedding, Emma decided to tackle Red Mountain, presumably to find a nice spot for a pre-wedding selfie. Guided by what she claimed was a Native American spirit guide—because who wouldn't want to take directional advice from an apparition?—she began her ascent. Sadly, it was during this hike that the second wave of her illness struck, knocking her off her feet and leaving her lifeless on the mountain.

With the gusto of a team of Olympians, Emma's fiancé and eleven other men, fueled by love and sheer determination, carried her casket up the mountain to give her a proper send-off. They clearly had not taken the time to read the fine print about permits, because who needs paperwork when love is on the line? They made it to the summit with all the flair of a high school prom committee, determined to honor her memory in style. However, as fate would have it, nature had other plans. A sudden flood caused a landslide that sent her casket tumbling back down to town, much like that time you tried to show off at the bowling alley and ended up bowling a strike in reverse—an impressive but wholly unexpected turn of events.

Undeterred, the townsfolk retrieved Emma's casket, which had become the unintentional star of a local episode of "Extreme Casket Retrieval." But even in death, Emma continued to have a knack for dramatic entrances. Over the years, pieces of her remains began turning up around town, like an eerie scavenger hunt that no one wanted to win. Locals would jokingly say, "If you find Emma's skull, you get a free mineral bath!" Though morbid, this turned into a running gag that added a twist of humor to an otherwise somber tale. Eventually, her skull was discovered, followed by other remnants, and Emma's remains found a more permanent resting place at the nearby Crystal Valley Cemetery.

Despite her tragic fate, Emma Crawford didn't fade away into obscurity; instead, she became a beloved local legend. The town commemorates her unique story with the annual Emma Crawford Coffin Races—a quirky celebration where participants decorate coffins and race them down the streets of Manitou Springs. Picture it: coffins zooming past cheering crowds while the smell of popcorn and roasted corn wafts through the air. It's a surreal combination of festive and macabre that has become a treasured local tradition.

Emma's story serves as a reminder that life is unpredictable and sometimes hilariously absurd, even when it involves a tragic end. From the heights of Red Mountain to the depths of the town's history, her journey is woven into the fabric of Manitou Springs, a testament to the belief that even in the face of misfortune, laughter and love can thrive. After all, if

Emma could have a coffin race in her honor, surely we can laugh a little at the absurdity of life and death, especially in a town that knows how to turn even the most somber tales into a grand celebration.

The Haunting of Riverdale Road

Nestled in the heart of Adams County, Colorado, lies an unassuming 11-mile stretch of pavement known as Riverdale Road, connecting the bustling towns of Thornton and Brighton. To the average driver, it might seem like just another route for your daily commute, a scenic drive with occasional glimpses of the majestic Rocky Mountains. However, for those brave enough to venture down this eerie roadway after dark, Riverdale Road has earned its reputation as one of the most haunted roads in the United States—unless you ask your skeptical friend who just thinks it's a glorified urban myth, in which case it's "just a bumpy ride with an interesting backstory."

As the sun dips below the horizon and the sky turns a dusky shade of blue, the air grows thick with stories that have been passed down through generations. The Denver Public Library has a whole section devoted to the legends that haunt this stretch of asphalt. Some locals swear they've seen a ghostly jogger who taps on the sides of passing cars, as if he's auditioning for the world's least effective exercise video: "Lose Weight by Haunting Your Neighbors." Imagine the scene: you're cruising along, and suddenly there's a ghostly figure running alongside your car, giving you the impression that you've just driven into an episode of *The Twilight Zone.*

Others recount chilling encounters with a phantom Camaro, notorious for its signature one headlight—perhaps it's just a classic case of "I only have enough energy for one eye" syndrome. Legend has it that the car appears out of nowhere, roaring up behind you before vanishing just as quickly, leaving you wondering if you should be terrified or amused. Maybe it's just a friendly ghost trying to share a ride, but you can't help but wonder how many times they've had to explain to confused drivers, "No, I'm not here for a real race, I just have a thing for dramatic entrances."

And let's not forget the infamous hitchhiker in white, who has a tendency to vanish into thin air before you can even ask, "Need a ride, or are you just here for the ambiance?" According to legend, if you pick her up, you may end up driving in circles for eternity, leading to some awkward conversations in the afterlife. "So, uh, do you come here often?" followed by an eerie silence. There's a fine line between giving a ride to a ghost and realizing you've just signed up for a never-ending road trip with someone who doesn't even pay for gas.

Among the myriad of legends that surround Riverdale Road, one story stands out like a classic horror film that you can't look away from: the fire at the David Wolpert House. Picture this: a cozy family home, the smell of dinner wafting through the air, children laughing, and then—bam! A fiery inferno of chaos. According to local lore, a man tragically set his house ablaze with his family still inside. As the flames roared and danced, the family perished, leaving the man to vanish without a trace, perhaps off to join a ghostly support group for arsonists with a penchant for the dramatic. Can you imagine the meeting? "Hi, I'm Bob, and I accidentally burned down my house… twice."

Yet, in a twist worthy of a soap opera, the Denver Public Library dug deeper into the archives, only to find… no reports of fatalities associated with the house fire. Oops! It seems that while a mysterious fire adds great flair to a ghost story, the reality is often far less sensational. Perhaps the family went on a ghostly vacation, lounging in the spectral sun, sipping ectoplasmic piña coladas, while their former home became the star of its own horror movie. As the fire crackled and the night turned cold, did the residents merely transform into ethereal entities, destined to haunt the very place where they lived? You can almost picture them lounging around, half-heartedly waving at passing cars, trying to figure out how to make a ghostly entrance without spilling their ghostly drinks.

For those brave enough to traverse Riverdale Road, it's a wild ride that defies reality and blends the mundane with the supernatural. The stories of lost souls and phantom vehicles create an atmosphere thick with intrigue and a hint of mischief, making it a favorite spot for thrill-seekers and paranormal enthusiasts alike. And while skeptics might roll their eyes, you can't deny that there's a certain charm to the idea of a ghostly jogger, a phantom Camaro, and an ever-elusive hitchhiker adding a bit of excitement to what could otherwise be just another boring drive.

As you cruise down Riverdale Road—perhaps late at night, fueled by a mix of curiosity and a slightly questionable playlist—don't be surprised if you catch a glimpse of something out of the ordinary. After all, in a place where legends live on, the line between reality and myth is as blurred as a foggy windshield on a chilly Colorado night. Who knows, you might just end up with a ghost story of your own. Just remember to keep your windows rolled down; the last thing you want is a tap-tap-tap on the glass from a jogger who forgot his running shoes.

But don't fret! As you navigate this haunted stretch of road, you might even consider adopting a new mantra: "When in doubt, honk it out!" After all, you never know when a spectral jogger might need a ride, or a phantom Camaro might want to join in on the fun. Just make sure you've got a good excuse ready when the ghostly hitchhiker asks why you're taking the long way home. After all, you're just a driver caught in the web of Colorado's most notorious ghost stories, trying to figure out if it's the eerie ambiance or the actual ghosts that make Riverdale Road so unforgettable.

The Last Stand of the Last Grizzly

Once upon a time, in the rugged mountains of Colorado, grizzly bears were as common as overpriced lattes in Boulder or the inevitable traffic jam on I-25. These magnificent beasts roamed the high country, occasionally stopping to ponder the meaning of life or munch on a wayward hiker's trail mix. However, as the years rolled by, grizzlies became a rare sight, much like a unicorn in a traffic jam—beautiful but not exactly practical. Fast forward to 1979, and the last grizzly bear in Colorado was about to make a memorable exit from the stage of wildlife history.

Our story begins on a crisp autumn day, when a man named Ed Wiseman ventured into the backcountry near the Continental Divide in the San Juan Mountains. Ed was a hunter, but that day, he was more like an overzealous tourist armed with a bow and a perhaps too-optimistic view of his own survival skills. After a few hours of searching for deer, Ed stumbled upon a clearing that was probably best described as a bear's buffet. And wouldn't you know it? There, sitting proudly on a ridge, was the last grizzly bear Colorado would ever see—well, at least until the teddy bear industry got its act together.

Now, let's take a moment to appreciate the sheer irony of the situation. Ed was there to hunt, and here was this enormous creature, likely weighing between 300 and 450 pounds, just chilling and doing bear things. Ed, however, didn't get the memo that this bear was not in the mood for games. As he approached, he cornered the bear in such a way that one could only assume the bear was thinking, "Really, Ed? This is how it ends?"

The bear, in a fit of panic or maybe just sheer annoyance, decided it was time to assert its dominance. It lunged at Ed with all the ferocity of a disgruntled fast-food employee when you ask for extra pickles. Ed, caught off guard and apparently not one to back down from a challenge, did the only logical thing he could think of: he fought back.

Armed with nothing but a hand-held arrow (which, let's be honest, sounds like a terrible weapon against something that could literally crush a car), Ed started stabbing the bear. Yes, you read that right. He was fighting a bear with an arrow. If you've ever seen a bear up close, you'll know that this isn't exactly a recommended strategy. One can only imagine the scene: Ed, wildly flailing his arrow while yelling, "You picked the wrong hunter today, furball!"

Despite the overwhelming odds, Ed's tenacity paid off. After what felt like an epic duel straight out of an action movie, the bear finally stopped moving. In a moment of pure, unadulterated shock—because, really, how does one process that kind of encounter?—Ed staggered away, nursing his wounds. Sure, he was mauled, but he had the satisfaction of knowing he had faced down a grizzly, which was more than anyone could say back at the local diner.

As Ed eventually made his way back to civilization, exhausted and bleeding, he was greeted with the warm embrace of disbelief. When he recounted the tale of his epic showdown with the last grizzly bear, he could almost hear the collective eye-roll of the townsfolk. They couldn't fathom that a man could single-handedly take down a bear, let alone that he had actually seen one.

In an effort to validate Ed's claims, the locals subjected him to a lie detector test. Ed, shockingly, passed with flying colors. This was the moment he realized that perhaps, in the wild world of bear encounters, the only thing more astonishing than surviving was being believed afterward.

Now, if you're wondering how a man could get himself into such a wild situation, let's just say Ed was a quintessential outdoorsman—an archetype of that brave soul who believes that nature is more than a pretty postcard. He was the kind of guy who bought "survival kits" at yard sales and thought "bear-proof" meant simply wearing a brighter-colored shirt than the last guy who had the misfortune of running into one.

That afternoon, after doing battle with a bear and emerging triumphant (or at least with a story to tell), Ed would have likely made a beeline for the nearest tavern to regale anyone who would listen. "You won't believe what I just did!" he might have exclaimed, with a slight slur, after a few rounds.

"I just fought a bear with an arrow! That's right, an arrow!" And as the locals exchanged skeptical glances and sipped their beers, Ed would've just smiled, certain that he was now the most interesting man in the room—though perhaps the most bandaged, too.

And so, the legend of the last grizzly bear in Colorado was born—not just of the bear, but of the man who fought valiantly against it, armed with nothing but an arrow and an outrageous sense of bravery. But despite Ed's heroic antics, the grizzlies never returned to Colorado, leaving behind a haunting emptiness and the unmistakable aura of a tale that would be whispered through the ages, right alongside the lore of mythical beasts and the urban legends of that one guy who claims he wrestled an alligator at a state fair.

As years passed, Ed's encounter transformed into folklore, inspiring a generation of hunters and nature enthusiasts to ask themselves, "What if?" What if they, too, could one day encounter a bear and fight it with little more than sheer will and a hand-held arrow? However, after hearing Ed's tale, they all decided to stick to fishing instead. After all, the only thing that ever got hurt in fishing is the fish—and occasionally the angler's pride when that "whopper" turns out to be a twig.

The Colorado Cannibal - A Taste of Survival

Years ago in the rugged, untamed wilderness of Colorado, a man named Alfred Packer set out on an expedition that would go down in history—though not for the reasons you'd expect. Packer wasn't seeking fame or fortune. In fact, he wasn't even trying to become a household name. Yet here we are, more than a century later, still talking about him as the infamous Colorado Cannibal. If he were alive today, Packer might have found himself on a Food Network special, but back then, his culinary adventures were less "Iron Chef" and more "I'm starving, and desperate times call for desperate measures."

It all began in the winter of 1874, when Packer and five other brave (and apparently very unlucky) souls decided to trek toward Breckenridge in search of gold. Now, trekking through the Colorado Rockies in winter is an activity that could generously be described as "ill-advised," but these men, hardy pioneers as they were, figured they'd push through the snowdrifts and freezing winds to strike it rich. What they didn't count on, however, was that Mother Nature had other plans. And, as it turned out, those plans included sub-zero temperatures, impassable terrain, and an impromptu lesson in just how quickly things can go downhill when you're stranded in the mountains with dwindling supplies.

By springtime, Packer was the last man standing—or rather, the last man hobbling into the Los Pinos Indian Agency near Gunnison, looking worse for wear and with a story that sounded about as believable as a fish tale told after a few too many drinks. He claimed his companions had abandoned him, leaving him to fend for himself. You could almost picture him, shivering and disheveled, telling the story with a straight face as the locals eyed him with suspicion. But hey, stranger things had happened in the Old West, right?

Unfortunately for Packer, his initial tale didn't quite add up. For one, the local authorities were curious as to why he seemed surprisingly well-fed for a man who'd supposedly spent months wandering the wilderness alone. A series of increasingly wild stories followed, each with more twists and turns than a soap opera plot. At first, Packer said that one of the other men in the group had gone mad, attacking everyone in a desperate bid for survival. Packer, in this version of the story, was simply the last lucky soul who managed to escape the madness. A tragic tale, sure—but something still didn't sit right.

As time passed, more holes appeared in Packer's account, and the situation started to smell fishier than a can of sardines left in the sun. The truth, or at least something close to it, began to emerge. The weather had turned brutal, trapping the group in the mountains with no food and no hope of rescue. With their supplies long gone and starvation setting in, the men started dying one by one. What happened next was the stuff of horror stories, the kind you might tell around a campfire if you wanted to guarantee no one got a good night's sleep. The survivors, desperate and delirious, had resorted to cannibalism.

Now, you might be wondering how the group ended up in such a dire situation in the first place. Surely, they could have packed a few extra sandwiches or something, right? But alas, this was the 19th century, and long-term planning wasn't always a priority. Plus, the Rockies in winter aren't exactly known for their abundance of edible flora and fauna. When your options are slim and the only thing on the menu is a frozen boot, well, you start making choices you'd rather not discuss at Sunday dinner.

By the time only three men remained, things had taken a turn for the even worse (yes, it was possible). One of the survivors, perhaps seeing an opportunity to get a little more "protein" in his diet, shot and killed the other remaining person. At least, that's how Packer told it—because, of course, in his version of events, he was merely the innocent bystander in all of this. According to him, it was a kill-or-be-killed situation, and he had no choice but to defend himself. After dispatching the final member of the group, Packer did what any sensible person in his shoes would do: he packed up some of the meat for sustenance and made his way down the mountain.

When Packer was eventually arrested and tried, he was charged with murder. After all, someone had to be held accountable for what happened up there, and his story was about as airtight as a sieve. However, the charges were later downgraded to five counts of manslaughter—because apparently, when you're dealing with cannibalism in the 1800s, the legal system is just as confused as everyone else. Packer ended up serving time but was eventually paroled, much to the horror and fascination of everyone who had followed the case.

In the years that followed, Packer lived out the rest of his days in Deer Creek, Colorado, where one imagines he probably avoided potluck dinners and invitations to cookouts. He passed away in 1907, taking with him whatever really happened in those mountains. Was he a victim of circumstance, forced to do the unthinkable to survive? Or was there something more sinister at play, a darker truth that Packer kept hidden behind his shifting stories? We'll never know for sure, but one thing's certain: Alfred Packer's name will forever be associated with one of the strangest, and tastiest, chapters in Colorado history.

And so, the tale of the Colorado Cannibal endures—a cautionary story of survival, desperation, and the lengths people will go when faced with the unimaginable. As for Packer, well, he probably would have preferred a different kind of legacy. But hey, at least he's got one. Some people are remembered for their bravery, others for their ingenuity. And then there's Alfred Packer, forever remembered as the man who turned a mountain expedition into an all-you-can-eat buffet.

The Forgotten Depths of Spaulding's Cavern

In the sprawling sandstone wonderland of the Garden of the Gods, where the red rocks rise in otherworldly formations and tourists gather to snap the perfect photo of the famous Kissing Camels, a secret lies hidden. If you've been to this park, you've probably marveled at the way the rocks seem to defy gravity, balancing precariously as if the earth had no say in the matter. You've likely followed well-worn paths, possibly even dodged a yoga class or two in a meadow. But there's something here that few talk about, and even fewer have seen: Spaulding's Cavern, a piece of Colorado history that's as elusive as a snowball in July.

The story of Spaulding's Cavern begins in 1848, when Jacob Spaulding—an explorer with a keen sense of adventure and perhaps a bit of questionable judgment—stumbled upon the cavern while wandering through the rugged terrain of what would eventually become Garden of the Gods. Nestled in North Gateway Rock, not far from the Kissing Camels formation, the cave was a massive but narrow opening that beckoned to those brave enough to squeeze inside. The kind of place that looks like it could swallow you whole if you weren't paying attention, or if the rocks above decided they'd had enough of holding themselves together.

At the time, caves were something of a rarity in the region, and naturally, word of Spaulding's discovery spread. Back in the 19th century, when you couldn't simply watch a video of spelunking on YouTube, you had to experience the real thing. So, people came in droves. Explorers, adventurers, and undoubtedly a few thrill-seekers with more enthusiasm than sense made their way into the cavern, crawling into its narrow depths with lanterns and torches, hoping to see what mysteries it might hold. It quickly became a hotspot for those seeking a little danger alongside their scenic views. Why hike a nice, safe trail when you can shimmy your way through a potentially life-threatening cavern, right?

Spaulding's Cavern grew in popularity, with visitors carving their names into the rock as a testament to their bravery (or lack of impulse control). By the early 20th century, it had become a popular attraction for locals and tourists alike. But as more and more people ventured inside, a problem emerged: the rocks around the cavern were fragile, the result of thousands of years of erosion, and the constant foot traffic wasn't helping. The cavern was in danger of collapsing, and in a rare moment of foresight, local officials decided that maybe—just maybe—it wasn't a good idea to let people keep crawling into a ticking time bomb made of rock.

So, in the 1930s, the cavern was sealed for the first time, much to the disappointment of adventure junkies everywhere. The entrance was blocked, and signs were put up warning people to stay away. And for a while, that was the end of the story. Or so it seemed.

But here's the thing about nature: it has a funny way of doing whatever it wants, no matter what we humans think we're in control of. In 1963, Spaulding's Cavern decided it wasn't done just yet. Due to erosion—an old friend to the Colorado landscape—the cavern reopened itself, almost as if it was thumbing its nose at the idea of being sealed. Once again, brave (and probably slightly reckless) visitors ventured inside, leaving their signatures on the walls as if to say, "Yep, we made it, and we didn't die."

For a brief time, the cavern was open again, and it became something of a secret challenge for those who knew about it. It wasn't listed in any official guides, and there were no signs pointing the way. If you found Spaulding's Cavern, it was because you knew someone who knew someone who was willing to share the secret. The cave became a sort of hidden gem, passed down through whispers and local lore. If you made it inside, you became part of a very exclusive club—one that involved a lot of squeezing through narrow rock passages and a good bit of dirt under your nails.

But, as with all good things, the reopening didn't last long. Officials once again decided that perhaps a collapsing cavern wasn't the best thing to leave open to the public, and Spaulding's Cavern was sealed for a second time. This time, they meant business. They blocked the entrance more securely, determined that no one would venture inside again.

Now, here's where the humor kicks in. You'd think that sealing a cavern once would be enough, but no. It turns out that rocks, like rebellious teenagers, have a tendency to do the opposite of what you tell them. Sealed or not, Spaulding's Cavern has a bit of a mind of its own, and while the entrance is officially closed, there's always a possibility that it could reopen, as if to say, "Hey, remember me? Want to give it another go?"

To this day, Spaulding's Cavern remains sealed, though its legend lives on in the whispers of locals and the occasional mention in old guidebooks. Those who know the story still talk about it, wondering if one day the cave will make a grand reappearance. And who knows? Maybe it will. After all, it's defied closure before. In the meantime, the cavern sits quietly beneath the rock, a hidden chamber filled with the signatures of those who once dared to enter.

And what of the people who explored it all those years ago? Their names remain etched into the walls of the cave, frozen in time like a 19th-century guestbook. If Spaulding's Cavern ever opens up again, maybe you'll find them there, a reminder of a time when adventure meant crawling into a dark hole in the ground and hoping for the best. But until then, the cave remains sealed, its secrets tucked away beneath the Garden of the Gods, waiting for the next adventurer bold—or foolish—enough to find it.

The Haunting of Gold Camp Road

Colorado is a state painted with vibrant hues, from its purple mountain majesties to the golden grains of the plains. But it's not just the landscape that tells a colorful story—our history is rich with tales of the macabre and the supernatural. And few places capture this eerie essence as compellingly as Gold Camp Road. Tucked away near Colorado Springs, it seems like any other road at first glance, but beneath its seemingly tranquil surface lurks a sinister secret that has drawn the brave, the curious, and the foolhardy to its haunted embrace.

Gold Camp Road is infamous for being one of Colorado's most haunted locations. This winding path follows an old rail line that once transported miners to the gold-rich hills of Cripple Creek. The tunnels, originally constructed in the 1800s, hold more than just the weight of history; they carry the tragic echoes of lives lost in a harrowing fashion.

Picture this: As the sun dipped below the horizon, casting eerie shadows over the landscape, workers toiled inside the tunnels, their picks and shovels clanging against the rock. Yet, in a cruel twist of fate, one worker was trapped when a section of the tunnel collapsed, burying him alive. No dramatic last words, no grand finale—just a suffocating darkness and the heavy silence of the mountain swallowing him whole. Imagine the dread as the last breath escaped his lips, leaving behind a haunting stillness.

But that was just the beginning of Gold Camp Road's dark legacy. As if the fate of that unfortunate worker wasn't enough to chill your bones, tragedy struck again. A school bus carrying a group of unsuspecting orphans met a grisly end when the very same tunnel collapsed, burying them under tons of rock and dirt. The sound of laughter turned to screams, and the bus, once a vessel of hope and adventure, became a tomb. It's said that the last thing they heard was the thunderous rumble of the mountain's fury, followed by an eerie silence that still hangs in the air today.

After the children's tragic deaths, the third tunnel was hastily sealed off. But this act of closure did little to quiet the restless spirits that now roamed the road. Locals began to whisper about ghostly apparitions that wandered the path at night, their small forms appearing like fleeting shadows, accompanied by the sounds of distant giggles and cries for help that echoed through the trees. Even the bravest adventurers who dared to drive down Gold Camp Road reported hearing chilling echoes of laughter—an unsettling reminder of the lives cut short.

As you traverse this ominous stretch of asphalt, keep an eye out for the inexplicable phenomena that often accompany such places steeped in tragedy. Visitors have claimed to find tiny, dusty handprints mysteriously appearing on their cars, as if the spirits of the children are reaching out for companionship, perhaps hoping to find a friendly face to share their sorrow. Even more disconcerting, some have felt the unmistakable sensation of being pushed or scratched when no one else is around—just a playful ghostly poke or a sinister reminder of the afterlife's presence.

The skeptics might shrug it off as mere folklore, but those who have walked the haunted road know the truth: the spirits are not just figments of imagination. In fact, many have reported seeing dark figures lurking in the periphery, vanishing into the shadows before you can get a good look. You can almost picture them peering out from the trees, their hollow eyes fixated on the living—curious, yet eternally mournful.

As if to solidify its reputation, the atmosphere on Gold Camp Road can shift in an instant. One moment, you're cruising along, soaking in the beauty of the Colorado wilderness, and the next, the air turns frigid. You might find your breath visible in the cool night air, despite it being a balmy evening. You can almost hear the whispers of the past brushing against your ear, filling your mind with questions that you don't want to ask.

So, what do you think? Are the eerie legends of Gold Camp Road and the tragic deaths within the tunnels true? Or are they simply the imaginings of restless souls still tethered to this earthly plane? With each twist and turn, the line between history and legend blurs, and the thrill of the unknown saturates the air like a dense fog creeping over the landscape.

This seemingly ordinary road hides a haunting story that begs to be told. As you navigate its path, remember to keep your windows rolled up and your heart steady. You might find yourself haunted not just by the memories of those lost but by the echoes of their lives—stories lingering in the darkness, waiting to share their tales with anyone brave enough to listen.

In the depths of night, when the wind howls and the shadows dance, Gold Camp Road invites you into its haunting embrace. And if you happen to hear the laughter of children echoing through the trees, remember that some spirits don't want to be forgotten. They linger, searching for solace and connection, reminding us that even in death, the past refuses to fade quietly away.

The Angel of Shavano, A Legend in the Snow

Mount Shavano stands majestically in Colorado's Sawatch Range, rising above the Arkansas River Valley like a sentinel of the sky. At 14,229 feet, it's one of those mountains that challenges both seasoned hikers and starry-eyed tourists alike, beckoning them with promises of summit views and personal glory. But for locals and those in the know, Mount Shavano offers something much more: a yearly reminder that not all of nature's wonders can be explained by science and topography alone. Every spring, as the snow begins to melt and the mountain shakes off its wintry coat, a shape emerges on its eastern face. It's not just any shape, though. It's the form of an angel, arms outstretched, wings seemingly unfurled—a divine figure watching over the land below. This is the Angel of Shavano.

Now, for anyone passing through the Arkansas River Valley, it's easy to see why the Angel draws so much attention. She's dramatic, beautiful, and, if the lighting's just right, looks a bit like she might start floating down from the mountain at any moment. For those who grew up in the shadow of Shavano, however, the Angel is more than a pretty patch of snow. She's a symbol of something greater—of sacrifice, of friendship, of rain in times of drought. Of course, what exactly she symbolizes depends entirely on who you ask, because, like all good legends, the story of the Angel of Shavano changes with the teller.

Let's start with one of the most popular versions of the legend, the one that often gets passed around campfires or over pints at local breweries. This tale begins with Chief Shavano, a Ute leader known for his wisdom, strength, and connection to the land. He was, as the story goes, a man with deep ties to his people and to the spirits of the mountains. One day, his close friend, George Beckwith—a white settler with a rugged mustache and the kind of face you'd trust to wrangle a herd of cattle—fell gravely ill. Beckwith's health began to decline rapidly, despite the efforts of everyone around him. Faced with the impending death of his dear friend, Chief Shavano did what any legendary figure would do: he climbed to the top of Mount Shavano to pray.

There, under the open sky, surrounded by the stillness of the high alpine air, Shavano poured out his soul. He begged the spirits to save his friend, to show him a sign that Beckwith's life would be spared. And then, as if the mountain itself was listening, an angel appeared in the snow. Her figure stretched out across the mountain's face, wings wide, a divine message from the gods that all would be well. Miraculously, Beckwith recovered, and the angel has returned every year since, a symbol of friendship, faith, and, perhaps, the occasional snowstorm that really needs to take a breather.

That's one version of the story, anyway. It's the kind of tale that tugs at the heartstrings, conjures images of rugged men with bushy beards, and inspires locals to stare reverently up at the mountain's face each spring. But like all good legends, there's a second, darker tale—one that involves drought, sacrifice, and, well, a lot of tears.

In this other version of events, the Angel of Shavano wasn't always there. Long ago, when the land was dry and the crops were failing, the Ute people were faced with a crisis. The rivers had dwindled to mere trickles, the once-lush valleys were parched, and the people were desperate for rain. It's in moments like these that someone always has to do something drastic. Enter the Ute princess. No name has been preserved for her, which, if we're being honest, adds a certain mystique to the whole affair. She was young, beautiful, and, most importantly, selfless. Believing that only her life could appease the gods and bring rain to her people, she did what all tragic heroines do—she climbed to the summit of Mount Shavano, where she offered herself in sacrifice.

The story goes that as she lay down to die, the sky darkened, the wind picked up, and the heavens wept. Rain poured down in torrents, flooding the valleys, filling the rivers, and saving her people. In return for her sacrifice, the gods etched her image into the mountainside, immortalizing her in snow, her wings spread in eternal vigilance over the land. To this day, she appears every spring, a reminder of the princess who gave her life for her people, and a gentle nudge that we all might owe her a rain dance or two.

These stories have been passed down through generations, and though they differ in detail, they both share a common theme: the Angel of Shavano is more than just a coincidence of snow and rock. She's a symbol of something greater, of the forces of nature and fate that shape the world we live in. Whether you believe in her spiritual significance or just see her as a cool snow pattern, there's no denying that she holds a special place in the hearts of those who call this region home.

But before you get too swept away by all this angelic grandeur, let's remember one thing: we're in Colorado, where every mountain has at least three legends attached to it, and half of them were probably made up by someone after a particularly long winter. The Angel of Shavano is no exception. Some locals will swear that the angel brings good luck, while others insist that she's just there to remind them to break out the snow shovels. There's even a running joke in Salida that if you can't see the angel from town, it's because she's on vacation, probably off summiting other mountains just for the fun of it.

Today, the Angel of Shavano still draws visitors and hikers alike, though not all of them are aware of the stories behind the snow. For those who make the trek to the summit, the angel becomes more than just a distant figure in the snow—it's a reminder of the power of nature, of the mountains that hold their secrets close, and of the people who keep those secrets alive. And for the rest of us, she's a pretty great excuse to pull over on Highway 50, stare up at the mountain, and appreciate a little bit of Colorado legend in our otherwise mundane, snow-shoveling lives.

So, if you find yourself near Mount Shavano in the springtime, take a moment to look up. Maybe you'll see the angel. Maybe you'll feel the presence of a Ute princess or a spiritual guide. Or maybe you'll just realize that no matter how many legends get spun about this place, one thing's for sure—Colorado sure knows how to keep its mountains interesting. And if you don't see the angel right away, don't worry. Like all good legends, she tends to show up when you least expect her.

Butch Cassidy's Treasure Hunt that Never Ends

When you think of Butch Cassidy, a few things probably come to mind: Wild West outlaw, bank robber extraordinaire, leader of the infamous "Wild Bunch" gang, and—if you're a fan of 1960s cinema—probably Robert Redford's ruggedly handsome face. But what doesn't come up as often is Colorado. Sure, the wild tales of Cassidy and his gang tearing through Wyoming, Utah, and South America are well-known, but his connection to the Centennial State? That's where things get really interesting. And, as with all good outlaw stories, there's buried treasure involved.

Let's set the stage: It's the late 1800s. Butch Cassidy and his gang are riding high on a spree of successful bank and train robberies. They've pulled off heists that would make modern-day criminals look like amateurs. After one of these heists, Butch and the boys decided it might be a good idea to stash their loot somewhere safe—just in case things got too hot for them. That's how a certain stretch of land in El Paso County, Colorado, near the sleepy town of Monument, became the rumored resting place for $100,000 worth of stolen cash.

Now, $100,000 in the late 1800s was more than just a chunk of change. Adjusted for inflation, we're talking about over $3 million today. Yes, you read that right. Cassidy wasn't just hiding a few coins under a rock somewhere; he was burying a fortune that could make anyone today think seriously about ditching their 9-to-5 job to go full-time treasure hunting. (And don't think some haven't tried.)

But here's the rub: no one knows where it is. Not a single soul has managed to unearth Cassidy's legendary stash. The rumors, however, are plentiful. Some say the treasure lies somewhere near Monument Rock, a towering geological formation that's impossible to miss. Others think it's hidden in one of the many canyons or gulches that snake through the Front Range, places so remote that only a dedicated explorer—or an equally dedicated outlaw—could find them.

The real question is: why Monument? What was Butch Cassidy, a man who could have hidden his treasure in any number of wide-open, lawless territories, doing in El Paso County? Well, one theory suggests it wasn't Cassidy's first choice. See, as the story goes, Butch was making his way down from a job gone awry, looking for a place to lie low for a while. He was on his way to New Mexico, but he got wind that the law was closing in. With few options and a suspiciously large amount of stolen cash weighing him down, he made the split-second decision to stash the loot where it would be least expected—right under everyone's noses in Colorado.

It's easy to imagine Cassidy and his gang, spurred by urgency, riding through the ponderosa pines and sandstone bluffs of Monument. They probably found some remote spot, dug a quick hole, and buried their treasure with the intention of returning later to retrieve it. But, as with many good outlaw plans, something went wrong. Maybe they never got the chance to come back. Maybe Butch forgot exactly where he put it. Or maybe—and this is the part treasure hunters love to speculate about—he never intended to retrieve it at all, leaving a tantalizing mystery for future generations to unravel.

What makes the legend of Butch Cassidy's missing gold even more compelling is how oddly plausible it all is. There's nothing outlandish about the idea that an outlaw on the run could have buried his loot in an out-of-the-way location. And the fact that it's in El Paso County, rather than some remote desert, only adds to the appeal. Why wouldn't Cassidy pick a spot that didn't scream "criminal hideout"? Plus, let's not forget, Monument was a quieter place back then. If you wanted to hide $100,000 worth of loot, it was the perfect spot—halfway between the chaos of the Wild West and the budding civilization of Colorado Springs.

Since the treasure was supposedly buried, countless people have tried their luck at finding it. From the early 1900s to today, there's been a near-endless stream of adventurers, armed with little more than shovels and a dream, wandering the hills of Monument in search of Cassidy's fortune. Some have even brought in fancy modern gadgets, like metal detectors and ground-penetrating radar, only to come up empty-handed. In fact, the closest anyone has ever come to finding the loot is a few old coins and some bullet casings—both fascinating, sure, but hardly the multi-million-dollar payday everyone's hoping for.

One particularly persistent treasure hunter claimed in the 1970s that he had "definitive proof" of the treasure's location, but when he set off with his map and his gear, he returned with nothing but sore feet and an even sorer ego. Still, this hasn't stopped new generations of would-be fortune seekers from packing their bags, donning cowboy hats, and taking to the hills in search of that elusive payday.

But here's where things get interesting—and a bit humorous. The fact that no one has found Cassidy's stash hasn't deterred people in the slightest. In fact, if anything, it's only made the legend grow stronger. Each year, more folks convince themselves that *they* are the ones who will finally crack the mystery. There's something inherently funny about the idea that after more than a century of searching, with all the advancements in technology and all the supposed "leads," no one has managed to find a treasure buried by a man who didn't exactly have Google Maps at his disposal. And yet, hope springs eternal. Because, let's face it, the idea of stumbling upon a chest of gold and cash—worth millions today—is too good to pass up.

So, if you're ever in El Paso County, wandering through Monument, and you spot someone crouching down, furiously digging near a random boulder, give them a nod. They're just the latest in a long line of treasure hunters trying their luck. Who knows? Maybe they'll strike gold—or maybe they'll just find some rusty old can. Either way, the legend of Butch Cassidy's missing gold isn't going anywhere.

And if you happen to be one of those adventurous souls who wants to take up the hunt, just remember: Butch Cassidy was nothing if not clever. He wasn't going to make it easy for you. So pack your shovel, your patience, and maybe a sense of humor—because the Colorado mountains are full of surprises, but they don't give up their secrets easily.

The Rise and Fall of Buckskin Joe

In the heart of Colorado, where the mountains kiss the sky and the rivers sparkle like freshly polished gold, lies the ghost of a town once alive with laughter, ambition, and a fair bit of mischief. Buckskin Joe, or as the locals tried to fancy it up, Laurette, was once a bustling mining camp that danced with dreams of wealth. Today, however, it is but a whisper of its former self—a mere ghost town shadowed by its own grand history.

The story of Buckskin Joe begins in 1859, when a prospector named Mr. Phillips stumbled upon a mining claim. The man had more ambition than sense, and after eyeing the claim, he declared it lackluster and moved on faster than you can say "panning for gold." Little did he know, the universe had other plans. In a classic case of "finders keepers," his claim was snatched up by Joseph Higgenbottom, a man whose fashion sense leaned heavily on the buckskin look—imagine a cowboy who had mistaken a craft fair for a clothing store.

Higgenbottom, clearly a man of refined taste, traded his mining tools for a horse and a gun. He promptly relinquished his water rights to pay off a whiskey tab—because what could be more important than hydration, right?—and galloped off to chase the gold in the San Juan Mountains, leaving behind a camp that would soon attract miners like moths to a glittery flame.

By the spring of 1860, word spread faster than a prairie wildfire: gold had been found, and Buckskin Joe was about to become the hottest spot this side of the Rockies. Sluice boxes sprang up along Buckskin Creek as miners extracted gold like it was candy at a county fair. Those early days saw the old Spanish method of arrastra put to good use, followed by the construction of a mill that could crush the soft ore. It was the mining equivalent of upgrading from a flip phone to a smart device—a major leap forward.

As miners flooded into the camp, the population swelled from a handful of hopeful prospectors to a vibrant community of over 3,000 people. The locals, with their uncanny knack for creative naming, attempted to rename the place Laurette, after the two women who graced the camp—sisters Laura and Jeanette Dodge—but let's be real, Buckskin Joe was just too catchy to pass up.

By 1861, Buckskin Joe had evolved from a scrappy mining camp to a full-fledged town, boasting two hotels, fourteen stores, and even a bank! And who could forget the arrival of Horace and Augusta Tabor? This dynamic duo loaded their supplies and set up shop in Buckskin Joe, quickly turning their store into the local success story. Horace, not one to shy away from responsibility, became the postmaster while

Augusta ran the post office. It's a bit ironic that a woman who couldn't legally hold that position was nonetheless the one keeping the town connected to the outside world.

Life in Buckskin Joe wasn't all gold dust and whiskey; it had its fair share of eccentricity. Take Father John L. Dyer, for example, a Methodist preacher who didn't just preach—he prospected! Between delivering sermons, he would cart mail across the snowy terrain on ten-foot-long skis, his pockets full of holy missives and a heart full of zeal. Dyer was like the original Colorado mailman, trudging through deep snow, his skis cutting a path where others dared not tread, carrying not just letters but hope, as he climbed over the passes like an alpine Santa Claus.

In January 1862, the Park County Seat waltzed its way from Tarryall to Buckskin Joe, claiming the spot like a shiny new trophy. But, as with many good things, this golden era couldn't last forever. By 1866, the gold deposits dwindled faster than a good whiskey at a saloon, and the courthouse made a one-way trip to Fairplay, leaving behind a town that would soon be in the throes of decline.

Even as the last saloons and gambling halls shuttered their doors, a few stubborn souls remained. J.P. Stansell found a way to profit off the remnants of the Phillips Mine, mining long after others had left for greener pastures. And Horace Tabor, who had transformed from a shopkeeper to a mining mogul, would soon make headlines in Leadville.

Today, if you wander the site of old Buckskin Joe, all that remains is a cemetery that tells the tale of those who once thrived in the now-silent town. The tombstones are a poignant reminder of the struggle and determination of those early miners and settlers. The grave of young Thomas Fahey, for instance, is a testament to the risks of mining life; he left his cabin on a blustery February day and was not seen again until June—like a delayed bus service but much, much worse.

Many of the graves belong to immigrants who ventured from distant lands, their headstones adorned with symbols of home, while the delicate craftsmanship speaks of lives once lived with joy and sorrow. It's hard to imagine that this quiet resting place was once filled with the raucous sounds of a thriving community, where gold fever drove men to do both remarkable and regrettable things.

Nestled on Highway 9, just northwest of Fairplay, Buckskin Joe's ghost town is a historical snapshot that captures the essence of Colorado's mining legacy. It's a place where the spirit of adventure mingles with the whispers of the past, and every step taken among the graves is a step back in time—a ghostly journey through an era of dreams, disappointments, and a good deal of whiskey-fueled antics.

So, whether you're a history buff, a ghost hunter, or just someone who enjoys a good story, Buckskin Joe has plenty to offer. Just be careful where you step; you never know who—or what—might be watching from the shadows of its storied past.

The Legend of Miss Silver Heels

In the last chapter I told you about Buckskin Joe, but from Buckskin grew another legend. A local hero emerged from the shadows of the dance hall—her real name was never known, but the miners dubbed her **Silver Heels.** The year was 1861, and she arrived in a flurry of stagecoach dust, leaving an imprint on the hearts (and quite possibly the pocketbooks) of every miner in the camp.

With legs that seemed to stretch on forever and a smile bright enough to light up the darkest mine shaft, Silver Heels was the belle of Buckskin Joe. The moment she stepped onto the creaky wooden stage in her dazzling dance shoes, the miners were entranced. They could hardly remember their gold pans, much less the gold itself; after all, why bother digging for gold when you could simply shower Silver Heels with gifts? It was as if a siren had landed in the midst of their dusty existence, and they were all too eager to toss their riches at her feet—probably not the most practical investment strategy, but who were we to judge?

Despite her initial plans to make a quick exit after a few performances, the camp had other ideas. The miners rallied together, begging her to stay with a fervor that could rival the most passionate of romances. "Please, Silver Heels!" they cried, tossing hats in the air and even offering to name a mountain after her. Because nothing says "we love you" quite like a towering peak, right?

So, Silver Heels decided to stay, and as a token of their gratitude, the locals named a mountain **Mount Silver Heels** in her honor. The mountain loomed proudly over the camp, its peaks almost as enchanting as its namesake, though probably a bit less delicate in nature.

But like many legends, the tale of Silver Heels has its haunting side. According to local lore, her spirit has never truly left the mining camp. For over a century, townsfolk have whispered about a heavily veiled woman dressed in black wandering through the cemetery, her presence felt but seldom seen. Carrying flowers—likely for all those poor souls who succumbed to the harsh realities of mining life—she glides silently through the graves, a sorrowful reminder of the beauty that once captivated the camp. The townsfolk joke that if you see her, you better bring a nice bouquet or risk being told off by a ghost in a bad mood.

But there's more to this story than just a pretty ghost. The legend of **J. Dawson Hidgepath**, a man whose aspirations were as high as the mountains, adds another layer of intrigue to Buckskin Joe's colorful history. Dawson arrived in Fairplay with dreams of striking it rich and finding a lovely bride, but instead, he met tragedy head-on—quite literally. In July 1865, Dawson took a tumble off Mount Boss while prospecting for gold. Sadly, the only thing he struck was the ground, and it was a hard landing.

After Dawson's untimely demise, the townspeople thought it was the end of the line for his story. But in the most bizarre turn of events, his bones were later found in a rather compromising position—on the bed of a prostitute in Alma. Now, some might chalk this up to a tasteless prank, but for the good folks of Buckskin Joe, this was just another day in the wild West.

Once the townsfolk reburied Dawson's remains in Buckskin Joe Cemetery, they probably thought they'd finally put the matter to rest. But much like that stubborn last slice of pie at Thanksgiving, Dawson's bones had a way of sticking around. Time and again, they found themselves back where they didn't belong—at the house of some unsuspecting "fair lady." By 1872, Dawson's bones were more famous than the local newspaper, earning a reputation that even the saloons couldn't compete with. People were tossing his bones down outhouses just to rid themselves of the pesky presence that refused to stay buried.

Now, if you think Dawson's shenanigans are wild, wait until you hear about the smallpox epidemic that swept through Buckskin Joe in the winter of 1861. Like a bad plot twist, the disease invaded the camp, leaving the miners and their families bedridden and desperately ill. As the rutted dirt road to the cemetery became a grim procession route, Silver Heels rose to the occasion. With her beauty and compassion, she transformed from a dance hall darling to a makeshift nurse, bravely tending to the sick and burying the dead as though she were auditioning for a role in a very macabre version of *Little House on the Prairie.*

The townsfolk sent messages to Denver pleading for help, but the only response was silence—perhaps the nurses were too busy fighting over who would get to wear the coveted white cap. With no one else to turn to, Silver Heels flitted from cabin to cabin, offering solace to the afflicted. She became a comforting presence in the chaos, nursing families back to health and providing comfort where there was little to be found.

When the worst of the epidemic finally passed by spring 1862, Silver Heels vanished as mysteriously as she had arrived. Some speculated she had contracted smallpox herself, leaving her once-beautiful face forever scarred. The miners searched high and low, but she was nowhere to be found. Rumors circulated that she had slipped away quietly, leaving behind a legacy of love and bravery—though many believe she still roams the cemetery, carrying flowers and mourning those who passed too soon.

Today, when you visit the Buckskin Joe Cemetery, you can almost hear the echoes of laughter and sadness mingling together. Perhaps if you listen closely, you might just catch a glimpse of a veiled woman in black, flowers in hand, or even the playful banter of Dawson's bones making a reappearance in the most unlikely of places. Whether or not these tales are true, they remind us that Buckskin Joe is more than just a ghost town; it's a place where history lingers in the air, leaving behind whispers of love, loss, and a few good laughs—often in the most unexpected of ways.

The Lafayette Vampire - Flu Vs. Folklore

Lafayette, Colorado—a town known more for its cozy neighborhoods and scenic foothills than anything spooky—holds a secret so strange, so eerie, that you might just find yourself rethinking that peaceful sunset stroll through its quiet cemetery. Sure, this is no Transylvania, but the residents of this unassuming town have an oddly famous neighbor—one who hails from the Carpathian Mountains and, according to local lore, might have fangs. Welcome to the story of Theodore Fodor Glava, or maybe it's John Trandifir. Honestly, the identity of Lafayette's infamous "vampire" is as foggy as a graveyard at midnight, but that only adds to the charm, right?

Let's rewind to 1918, a year when the Spanish Flu was wreaking havoc across the globe. People were dropping like flies, and medical science was just starting to grapple with the idea of washing hands. Into this chaotic scene strolled Theodore Fodor Glava—27 years old, newly arrived from Transylvania (yes, *that* Transylvania), and ready to start a new life in the American West. Except fate, as it tends to do in these kinds of stories, had other plans. Theodore fell victim to the flu and was buried in Lafayette Municipal Cemetery, where one might assume his story would end. But if that were the case, you wouldn't be reading this, now would you?

The trouble began after his death, when strange things started happening around Theodore's grave. Local legend has it that a tree—a very specific tree—began to grow out of the soil above his resting place. That's right: a tree, sprouting from the grave of a man from Transylvania. Now, you could be forgiven for thinking that trees grow from all sorts of places, but this particular tree was different. For one, it wasn't supposed to be there, as if the earth itself couldn't help but sprout something supernatural. And two, it grew right through the middle of Theodore's grave—right where his heart would've been.

Enter the local folklore. You see, in the vampire-hunting playbook, there's a rather specific way to ensure the undead stay, well, dead. You drive a wooden stake through their heart. Simple, effective, and apparently something the good folks of Lafayette decided to try. According to the story, a stake had been driven into Theodore's chest before burial, and from that stake, the tree grew—nourished by the blood of the supposed vampire beneath. Whether this stake was precautionary or someone had inside knowledge of Theodore's nighttime activities, we'll never know. But one thing's for certain: a creepy tree sprouting from a

Transylvanian's grave is enough to get the rumor mill turning.

Of course, in a small town like Lafayette, tales of vampires don't stay quiet for long. Soon, reports of strange occurrences around Theodore's grave began to pile up. Visitors claimed to hear disembodied whispers as they walked past. Some swore they saw lights flickering among the headstones late at night, while others felt an inexplicable chill in the air whenever they neared the site. The real kicker came from local paranormal investigator Drea Penndragon—because let's face it, if your name is Penndragon, ghost hunting is probably in your job description.

Armed with her ghost-hunting gadgets and an eagerness to crack the case, Drea visited the grave and was greeted by a chilling message: "Do you want to see my stake?" Now, I'm not saying vampires have a flair for the dramatic, but if I were one, this is exactly the kind of thing I'd say to mess with visitors. Whether it was a spirit from beyond the grave or just the wind playing tricks, the message was enough to send shivers down the spines of even the most skeptical investigators.

But was Theodore really a vampire, or was he just an unlucky immigrant caught up in a flu epidemic at the wrong place and time? The answer depends on whom you ask. There are no records of Theodore rising from the dead to haunt the townspeople, nor are there any confirmed sightings of him lurking in the shadows with blood on his lips. But that hasn't stopped the legend from growing over the years.

In fact, Theodore's grave has become something of a local attraction. Curious ghost hunters, thrill-seekers, and tourists with a taste for the macabre make their way to Lafayette Municipal Cemetery, hoping to catch a glimpse of the otherworldly. Some swear they can feel an energy around the grave, a kind of pull that beckons them closer. Others come armed with garlic, just in case.

The tree, which was once the central feature of the legend, no longer stands—it was cut down sometime in the mid-20th century, presumably by someone who didn't appreciate the idea of a vampire-infested arboretum. But the stories live on. To this day, people report strange happenings around Theodore's final resting place. Some claim to have seen shadowy figures moving among the headstones, while others report hearing a distant, disembodied voice asking them the all-important question: "Do you want to see my stake?"

Let's pause for a moment. You might be asking yourself, "Why Lafayette? Why, out of all places in the world, would a vampire show up in Colorado?" Well, if you think about it, Colorado isn't such a bad spot for the undead. The air is thin, so if you're used to being light on your feet (or your wings), the altitude wouldn't be much of an issue. Plus, the nights are long in the winter, which gives vampires ample time to go about their nocturnal activities. And let's not forget: the Rockies make for great hiding places. If you're a vampire in need of some downtime, Colorado offers plenty of options.

But let's be real. The most likely explanation for all this vampire business is that Theodore Fodor Glava—or John Trandifir, depending on which side of the headstone you're on—was just an unfortunate guy who died young and left behind a fertile plot of land. The tree? Well, trees grow in cemeteries all the time. As for the stake? Maybe it was just a coincidental sapling. But where's the fun in that?

So here we are, over a century later, still talking about a man whose only crime might have been catching a bad case of the flu. Maybe Theodore wasn't a vampire. Maybe he was just a regular guy who met an untimely end. Or maybe, just maybe, Lafayette's quiet municipal cemetery hides a secret darker than we'll ever know. One thing's for sure: the next time you find yourself wandering through a graveyard at dusk, keep an eye out for strange lights, listen for soft whispers on the wind, and, for heaven's sake, don't accept any invitations to see someone's stake. It's just common sense.

The Ghost Train of Marshall Pass

Picture this: the majestic peaks of Colorado loom overhead as you, Nelson Edwards, an old railroad engineer with more stories than teeth, find yourself perched in the cab of your trusty locomotive. It's a chilly night in 1880, and you're about to embark on another run over Marshall Pass, which, let's be honest, sounds like a lovely place until you realize it's twelve thousand feet above sea level. Just a casual stroll, right? Well, except for the fact that the *only* path involves a train and an absurd amount of mountain snow.

After a couple of months of successfully transporting passengers without any hitches (or *wrecks*, as you call them), you're feeling pretty good about your skills. That is until tonight, when a foreboding chill settles over the canyon. It's deeper, darker, and frostier than a snowman's refrigerator.

Now, earlier that day, someone—probably the same person who brought a pet iguana to a bar—reported a defective rail and an unsafe bridge. But hey, what's a little danger to a seasoned engineer? Just your everyday Tuesday! You've never met an unsafe bridge you couldn't cross… until now. As you start the long, nerve-wracking ascent, you hear a whistle echoing ominously in the distance. Just as you're about to roll up your sleeves and tackle this train like it's a stubborn mule, the *gong* in your cab sounds. Well, that's not good.

In a fit of panic, you apply the brakes. Before you can even finish processing what's happening, your conductor bolts up to you, a look of confusion on his face. "What did you stop for?" he asks, hands on his hips.

"Why did you signal to stop?" you shoot back, eyebrows raised.

"I gave no signal!" He looks like he's about to break into a rendition of "The Sound of Silence." "Pull her open and light out! We've got to pass No. 19 at the switches, and there's a wild train climbing behind us!"

A wild train? As if this night couldn't get any better! The sort of news that would make even a caffeine-fueled squirrel shudder. With a resigned sigh, you draw the lever, sand the track like a maniac, and get the train rolling again.

But wait! The whistles behind you grow closer. *A mad engineer is driving the train behind you?* Just when you thought you were the craziest person on this mountain! As you round a curve, you glance back, and what do you see? A train hot on your heels, an engineer leaning out the window with a grin that could only be described as "made of dough." Seriously, is it too late to quit this job?

The snow starts drifting in the hollows like an overeager dog flinging itself into a snow pile, and the train rumbles onward. Bridges quake beneath you as you thunder across, and the wind screams in your ears like a banshee auditioning for a horror movie. But you push on, heart racing, as the dreaded bridge looms ahead. Your heart is pounding louder than a kid on Christmas morning. Just as you cross it, you feel like an Olympic athlete clearing a hurdle.

But wait—*what's this?* You notice the switch up ahead, and a red light swinging like a wild pendulum signals impending doom. The train behind you is practically breathing down your neck. Time for some quick decision-making! With a *reverse* of the lever, you slam on the brakes and embrace a moment of pure dread.

No sound follows. Heart pounding, you look back just in time to see the wild train leap onto your own—just kidding! The tracks seem to part like the Red Sea, the engine topples off the bank, and the whole shebang rolls into the canyon below.

Well, that's new. You shudder and hold your breath, expecting the sound of splintering wood and cries of anguish. Instead, all you hear is the wind howling through the black abyss, making it sound like the world just lost a really bad singing competition.

With the lantern ahead now vanished, you've got to make a run for it. No time to linger—after all, No. 19 could be right behind you! You kick your engine back into high gear and race towards the second switch, where you arrive just in time to save your own skin.

Once you reach Green River—bright-eyed and bushy-tailed—you notice a mysterious message written in the frost of your cab window: "A frate train was recked as yu saw. Now that yu saw it yu will never make another run. The enjine was not ounder control and four sexshun men wor killed. If yu ever run on this road again yu will be recked."

Okay, *that's* not ominous at all. More like a poorly written horror film script. After reading that, you promptly decide that your train-running days are over, and you march straight back to Denver, vowing never to step foot on a train again—unless it's to ride in a passenger car with a cocktail in hand.

So there you have it, folks: no wreck was ever discovered the next day in the canyon where you'd witnessed that phantom train vanish. And to this day, not a single engineer has dared to cross Marshall Pass again without thinking twice about the wild train chase that never was… or was it?

Perhaps the next time you're up in the mountains, you might just hear the echoes of a long-lost train on a frosty night, bringing with it the thrill of the unknown and a hint of adventure. Or, at the very least, the perfect excuse to stay in and binge-watch your favorite show instead.

Tommyknockers - Colorado's Creepy Miners

The hills and mountains of Colorado aren't just filled with gold, silver, and precious minerals. They're also packed with tales of strange, mysterious creatures who made life just a little more interesting for the miners who braved the deep, dark shafts. And no story was quite as beloved (or feared) as the one about the Tommyknockers. Picture this: you're a grizzled 19th-century miner, covered in soot and sweat, about to head deep into the bowels of a Colorado mountain. You've got your pickaxe in hand, a lantern barely cutting through the pitch-black darkness, and then you hear it—a faint, rhythmic knocking from the walls of the cavern.

Relax! That's just your friendly neighborhood Tommyknocker.

Tommyknockers were said to be tiny men—green, wrinkled, and not exactly winning any beauty contests—who made their homes deep inside Colorado's mines. These miniature mischief-makers were more than just a figment of miners' imaginations, though. To the men spending hours (sometimes days) underground, the Tommyknockers were part guardian angel, part mischievous troublemaker, and a whole lot of "you better show some respect, or else."

Legend has it that if the Tommyknockers liked you, they'd tap along the cavern walls to warn you of danger. Maybe a tunnel was about to collapse, or some dynamite was a little too close for comfort. Those mysterious knocks, echoing through the rock, were a sure sign that you were in the Tommyknockers' good graces. And in a profession where danger was always just a heartbeat away, having a supernatural safety team on your side was no small thing.

But, of course, there was a catch. Tommyknockers weren't just there to be helpful—they were there to be appeased. Forget your manners, steal someone's lunch, or, heaven forbid, insult the little guys, and they'd turn on you faster than you could swing your pickaxe. The knocking would stop, the Tommyknockers would vanish, and suddenly, your day at the mine went from bad to worse. No miner worth his salt wanted to work in a silent mine. Silence meant that the Tommyknockers had left, and when they left, bad luck followed.

You see, the Tommyknockers had their own code of conduct. Treat them well, leave a bit of food or drink as an offering, and they'd look out for you and your fellow miners. Disrespect them, and they'd sabotage your equipment, hide your tools, or, in extreme cases, cause accidents. And while no miner ever actually *saw* a Tommyknocker, you better believe they were real. At least, that's what every miner in Colorado swore up and down.

The legend of the Tommyknockers was so deeply ingrained in mining culture that even long after a mine closed, the shafts weren't always sealed up completely. After all, it would be rude to trap the Tommyknockers inside, right? Instead, they were given an escape route, so they could follow the miners to their next job—or haunt the place for eternity. Whichever came first.

One of the hot spots for Tommyknocker activity was the old mining town of Leadville. Back in its heyday, Leadville was booming with silver mines, saloons, and a never-ending stream of hopeful prospectors looking to strike it rich. And where there were mines, there were Tommyknockers, tapping away to make sure their favorite miners didn't meet an untimely end.

Leadville's miners were particularly protective of their little green friends. Miners would leave the last bite of their lunch, usually a corner of a sandwich or a slice of pie, as a thank-you offering to the Tommyknockers. As the saying went, "A fed Tommyknocker is a happy Tommyknocker." And trust me, no one wanted an angry Tommyknocker in their mine. There were even reports of miners swearing they'd been saved by the Tommyknockers, hearing the telltale knocks just moments before a cave-in.

In nearby Telluride, another legendary mining town, the Tommyknockers were equally active. Miners there swore that on more than one occasion, the Tommyknockers had led them to veins of precious silver—often just after playing a few pranks. One miner famously claimed that he followed the sound of knocking only to find his missing pickaxe wedged in the rock, precisely where the richest silver seam was hiding. Coincidence? The miners didn't think so.

The Tommyknockers' origins are a bit murky, but many believe the legend came over with Cornish miners who immigrated to the U.S. during the 19th century. In Cornwall, England, miners had long told tales of similar creatures called "knockers" who haunted the tin mines. When these miners came to Colorado in search of work, they brought their superstitions—and their invisible friends—along with them. The American miners were only too happy to adopt the story, adding a bit of Colorado flair and turning the Tommyknockers into a local legend.

Of course, as with any good ghost story, there's always the question of whether or not the Tommyknockers were real. Skeptics will say that the knocking sounds were nothing more than the natural creaks and groans of the earth. Maybe it was the sound of pressure shifting in the rock, or wind howling through the shafts. But to the miners who spent day after day in those dark, damp tunnels, the Tommyknockers were as real as the gold they were digging for.

And it wasn't just the miners who believed. Local townsfolk would occasionally hear the Tommyknockers themselves, tapping away beneath their feet as they went about their daily lives. In some cases, entire towns would refuse to build over old mine shafts, fearing that the Tommyknockers would curse any structure placed above their underground domain.

To this day, Colorado's mining towns still tell stories of the Tommyknockers. While the mines may have long since shut down, the legend persists. Ghost tours through places like Leadville and Cripple Creek often include a mention of the mysterious little men, and visitors to old mining sites are told to listen closely for the faint sound of knocking in the distance.

Maybe it's just an old tale passed down through generations of miners, or maybe the Tommyknockers are still out there, keeping a watchful eye on Colorado's mountains, ready to knock whenever they're needed most. So, the next time you find yourself in one of the state's historic mining towns, take a moment to listen. If you hear a soft knock echoing from the rock, don't be alarmed. Just be grateful that the Tommyknockers are still on duty, keeping Colorado's mountains safe—one knock at a time.

And maybe, just maybe, leave them a slice of pie. Just in case.

Stanley Hotel Ghost Legends

Nestled in the scenic town of Estes Park, Colorado, where the mountain air is crisp and the elk roam free (sometimes right into your front yard), stands the Stanley Hotel. It's big, it's beautiful, and it's famously haunted. In fact, it's so haunted that it's become one of the most famous ghost-infested locations in the United States. If you're a fan of the paranormal, this is pretty much the Disneyland of ghostly activity—minus the mouse ears and plus a whole lot more piano-playing specters.

You may have heard of the Stanley Hotel before, especially if you're a fan of Stephen King's spine-chilling novel *The Shining.* That's right—this is *the* hotel that inspired King to create one of the most famous horror stories of all time. It's the place where "Heeeere's Johnny!" was born, and if you ask nicely (or not-so-nicely), you can still find plenty of people willing to tell you about all the weird things that go bump in the night. But while *The Shining* may have put the Stanley on the map, the hotel's ghost stories go way beyond King's terrifying tale.

The Stanley Hotel was built in 1909 by Freelan Oscar Stanley—yes, the same guy who co-invented the Stanley

Steamer, the early automobile that puffed and sputtered its way into the annals of history. The hotel was meant to be a peaceful retreat, a place where wealthy visitors could come to breathe in the fresh mountain air and relax. Little did Mr. Stanley know that over a century later, people would be coming to check in not for relaxation, but for a chance to share a room with a ghost. Ah, progress.

Let's start with one of the Stanley's most famous paranormal residents—Flora Stanley, Freelan's wife. Flora was a talented pianist, and it seems that even in the afterlife, she wasn't ready to give up her passion for tickling the ivories. Guests and staff alike have reported hearing the soft, eerie sound of a piano playing by itself in the hotel's concert hall. It's not just any tune, either—it's usually an elegant waltz, the kind you'd expect from a 1900s society lady who didn't let death stop her from getting in a few practice sessions. Now, if you hear it, don't worry. Flora's said to be a friendly ghost. Just don't ask her to take requests. She's dead, not Spotify.

And then there's the fourth floor—where things really get spooky. If you're feeling brave, you can book a room up there, though you might want to sleep with one eye open. Visitors staying on the fourth floor have reported all kinds of ghostly happenings. The most frequent sighting? Children. Ghost children, to be exact, which we all know is like twice as creepy as regular ghosts. Guests have claimed to hear the sounds of kids running through the halls, laughing and playing—except when they check the hallways, there's no one there. Whether these spectral kiddos are having a ghostly game of hide-and-seek or just trying to spook the living, one thing is certain: they know how to make an impression.

And then there's Room 217, possibly the most famous of all. This room is where Stephen King himself stayed during his visit to the Stanley Hotel, and it's where he got the inspiration for *The Shining.* But before King's terrifying visions, Room 217 had a bit of a frightful history of its own. In 1911, a housekeeper named Elizabeth Wilson was nearly killed when an explosion rocked the room. Miraculously, she survived, but the room hasn't been the same since. Guests have reported everything from their luggage being unpacked to mysterious cold drafts sweeping through the room. And sometimes, guests say they feel a gentle tuck-in sensation, as if Wilson's ghost is still making sure they're comfortable. You know, in that *creepy ghost housekeeper* kind of way.

But let's not forget the ghostly cowboys. Because, of course, no haunted hotel would be complete without a spectral cowboy. Guests have reported waking up in the middle of the night to find a cowboy sitting at the edge of their bed, watching them sleep. Most of the time, he just tips his hat and vanishes, which, let's be honest, is exactly what you'd want from a ghost cowboy. No need to overstay your welcome, sir. Thank you for the polite apparition, but maybe I'll switch hotels next time.

The Stanley Hotel has embraced its reputation as one of the most haunted places in the country, and why wouldn't they?

Where else can you get luxury accommodations *and* the possibility of seeing a piano play itself? They even offer ghost tours, so you can get a front-row seat to all the spooky shenanigans that make the Stanley so famous. Whether it's catching a glimpse of Flora at the piano or hearing the echo of ghostly footsteps in the halls, there's no shortage of eerie excitement.

So, what's the real deal with the Stanley Hotel? Is it truly haunted? Well, that depends on who you ask. Some people come to the Stanley and leave with spine-tingling stories of paranormal encounters. Others check out, having experienced nothing more frightening than a bad case of the breakfast buffet jitters. But one thing is certain: the Stanley Hotel has captured the imaginations of guests for over a century, and whether you believe in ghosts or not, it's hard to deny that the place has a certain… otherworldly charm.

Who knows? Maybe the next time you visit, you'll get a little piano concert from Flora, a ghostly cowboy tipping his hat, or even a midnight visit from those playful ghost kids on the fourth floor. Just remember, if things start to get a little too spooky, you can always do what Stephen King did—turn the experience into a bestselling novel.

That Time Colorado Springs Fell into Darkness

In the summer of 1899, Colorado Springs was a quiet town known more for its stunning mountain views than for being a beacon of scientific innovation. Little did anyone know that this sleepy town was about to become the stage for one of the most electrifying (literally) episodes in scientific history—thanks to none other than Nikola Tesla, the original mad scientist.

Tesla, best known today for inspiring electric car names and eccentric Halloween costumes, was, in fact, a bona fide genius. He had ideas that were ahead of his time—way ahead. Wireless electricity? Check. Earthquake machines? Sure, why not. And, of course, the infamous Tesla Coil, his crowning achievement in shooting lightning bolts just because he could. But before Tesla became a household name for creating electrical storms indoors, he was conducting mind-bending experiments in the scenic—and surprisingly accommodating—town of Colorado Springs.

Why Colorado Springs, you ask? Well, the town wasn't just pretty to look at; it had dry air (good for electricity), frequent lightning storms (good for inspiration), and, most importantly, a very generous city council. Tesla's charisma and promises of bringing the future to their little town earned him a sweet deal—free land and unlimited power. That's right. *Unlimited power*. It's almost like they handed him the keys to the Death Star and said, "Knock yourself out, buddy." Spoiler alert: He did.

With his new laboratory set up and a dream of harnessing the very forces of nature, Tesla wasted no time in getting to work. His goal? Nothing too ambitious, just creating his own lightning bolt. You know, casual Thursday stuff. The Tesla Coil, the device he'd been tinkering with for years, was finally ready for its big moment. And on one fateful day in July, he decided to unleash its full power.

As Tesla flipped the switch, the laboratory crackled to life. Electrical arcs shot from the coil, lighting up the room in a way that would make Dr. Frankenstein jealous. The air hummed with energy, and then, it happened: a massive lightning bolt shot out of Tesla's lab, stretching over 100 feet into the sky. It wasn't just any bolt; this was the mother of all lightning bolts, and the thunder it produced could be heard over 20 miles away in Cripple Creek. The town was in awe, and for a brief moment, Tesla must have felt like Zeus himself, tossing lightning bolts around like it was his day job.

Then the lights went out.

Tesla's grand experiment had created a literal power surge that knocked out electricity across the entire town of Colorado Springs. It wasn't just a flicker, either—this was an epic blackout. Homes, businesses, and even the streetlamps were plunged into darkness, with only the distant rumble of that enormous thunderclap as a reminder of what had just happened. Oh, and the small fact that Tesla's little experiment had also managed to set the local electric company's equipment on fire. Oops.

For the residents of Colorado Springs, this was probably not the "brighter future" they had envisioned when they gave Tesla free reign over their electricity. Imagine sitting down to dinner, candles lit, the soft glow of electric lamps filling your home—only to have everything suddenly go pitch black, and hearing the sound of distant thunder that isn't exactly coming from the sky. That's the moment when you realize you've put all your eggs in one very unstable, mad-scientist-shaped basket.

As you can probably guess, the local electric company was *not* pleased. Tesla had, in one fell swoop, managed to fry their entire power grid, which, let's be honest, is an impressive feat when you think about it. But here's the kicker—Tesla didn't even seem too bothered. He was on the verge of unlocking the secrets of the universe, after all. What's a little citywide blackout in the grand scheme of things?

Unfortunately for Tesla, the electric company saw things differently. They promptly cut him off. No more free electricity, no more supercharged experiments, and no more giant lightning bolts over the town. Tesla's lab, which had been his dream factory for creating the future, was torn down shortly after to help pay for the damaged generator. His brief reign as Colorado Springs' resident thunder god was over.

But the story doesn't end there. Despite the chaos and the blackouts, Tesla's time in Colorado Springs laid the groundwork for some of his most groundbreaking inventions. And the town, though it may not have appreciated having its lights knocked out, became an indelible part of the legend of Nikola Tesla—the man who quite literally brought darkness to a place so he could show it the light.

In the end, what did Colorado Springs get for its trouble? A good ghost story, a bit of scorched equipment, and a place in the annals of scientific history. As for Tesla, well, he went on to do more incredible things, and maybe—just maybe—he left behind a little of that electrical magic in the air of Colorado Springs. Either that, or it's just a coincidence that the lightning storms out there seem a little more… intense than elsewhere.

So, the next time you find yourself in the Pikes Peak region, take a moment to think about that time the entire town fell into darkness, all because of one man's dream to harness the power of the gods. And hey, if the lights start flickering? You can always blame Tesla.

Mysterious Deaths of San Luis Valley

If you think Colorado is all majestic mountains, craft beer, and happy ski bums, let me introduce you to a far less cheerful chapter of its history—one involving dead farm animals, mysterious circumstances, and some of the weirdest unsolved mysteries you've probably never heard of. Welcome to the San Luis Valley, where, in the 1960s, something very strange started happening.

Imagine you're a farmer in the wide, empty expanse of the San Luis Valley, a place so vast and open you could see a tumbleweed coming from three miles away. Your days are filled with the usual: feeding livestock, mending fences, and keeping an eye on the weather. All is well in your world until one day, you walk out to check on your herd and find… well, something you never expected.

One by one, farmers across the valley started discovering their animals—cows, sheep, even horses—dead in the fields. Now, dead animals on a farm aren't exactly out of the ordinary, but what made these cases bizarre were the details. These animals weren't just dead. They were, to put it lightly, *freakishly* dead. We're talking precision incisions, skin peeled off like someone was doing leatherwork on the fly, and various body parts missing. Oh, and here's the kicker—there wasn't a drop of blood anywhere to be found. Clean as a whistle. No tracks, no struggle, just a mystery that left everyone scratching their heads... and maybe checking over their shoulders.

Rumors spread faster than wildfire. Some said it was the work of a cult. Others were convinced aliens had landed and were using the livestock for some intergalactic science experiment. It was the 1960s, after all—UFO sightings were practically a weekend hobby, and the San Luis Valley was known as a hotbed for strange lights in the sky. Could it be that our friendly neighborhood extraterrestrials were into... cattle mutilation? Because apparently, probing just wasn't cutting it anymore.

Farmers weren't laughing, though. As more and more animals turned up dead in the same strange fashion, panic set in. It wasn't just that their prized livestock were being, well, dissected—it was the sheer weirdness of it all. No tracks, no signs of predators, and, again, *no blood*. For anyone who's ever butchered a cow (as one does), you know it's not exactly a neat and tidy process. The fact that these animals looked like they'd been handled by some sort of surgical team—but with none of the mess—had everyone spooked.

By the time the FBI got involved, this wasn't just a local mystery anymore. Similar incidents were popping up all over the country—Kansas, Minnesota, Nebraska. It was like some kind of national epidemic, except instead of the flu, we had what the papers started calling the "Cattle Mutilations." Great. As if farmers didn't have enough to worry about with droughts and market prices, now they had to deal with mysterious livestock murders.

Naturally, the FBI did what the FBI does—they launched an investigation, collected evidence, and came back with... well, nothing particularly satisfying. After examining over 100 incidents across nine states, their official conclusion was that the mutilations were the result of "natural causes." You know, like when coyotes just happen to peel back the skin with surgeon-like precision and drain every ounce of blood without leaving a mess. Totally natural.

Needless to say, the farmers weren't buying it. "Natural causes" felt about as believable as the idea that a flock of well-organized, highly trained birds had descended on the valley and decided to conduct their own bizarre little experiments. To this day, many of the locals still believe there's more to the story. Whether it was the work of a secret government program, a rogue scientist, or—let's not forget—the little green men from above, the San Luis Valley deaths remain one of Colorado's creepiest unsolved mysteries.

In the end, the case of the dead animals in the San Luis Valley is a lot like that one weird thing you swear happened when you were a kid—everyone has a theory, no one has proof, and the whole thing is just unsettling enough to make you think twice the next time you hear something go bump in the night. So, if you ever find yourself driving through the valley on a quiet evening, and you see a strange light hovering in the distance, just remember: it's probably nothing.

Probably.

The Truth Is Out There... in Hooper Colorado

Let me set the scene: you're on a road trip through the great state of Colorado, driving through the sprawling, eerily flat expanse of the San Luis Valley. The mountains loom in the distance, but right now it feels like you're the only soul for miles. The sun is setting, painting the sky in a palette of purples, oranges, and pinks, and you're on a mission. Not to visit some famous mountain or iconic ski resort, but to find UFOs. And where else would you go than Hooper, Colorado—a town that's become a hotspot for all things extraterrestrial, home to the famous UFO Watchtower?

Hooper is not exactly what you'd call a bustling metropolis. In fact, blink and you might miss it entirely, except for one curious landmark: a tall metal structure, standing like a sentry in the middle of nowhere, watching over the vast emptiness. This is the UFO Watchtower, and it's the perfect place for spotting those glowing orbs, mysterious flashes, and otherworldly visitors that people swear they've seen in the skies above the valley.

Now, if you're unfamiliar with the Watchtower, don't expect some high-tech NASA facility complete with radar equipment and government agents in dark suits. No, the Watchtower is more of a quirky, grassroots affair—a two-story metal observation deck with a gift shop. The gift shop, by the way, is stocked with just about everything a UFO enthusiast could need, from alien figurines to t-shirts that boldly declare, "I Want to Believe." The place feels like Area 51's laid-back cousin.

The thing is, folks in Hooper take their UFO sightings seriously. And why wouldn't they? According to local lore, strange lights and odd happenings have been reported in the San Luis Valley for decades. People claim to have seen everything from glowing orbs darting across the sky to inexplicable flashes of light. Some even swear they've seen full-blown spacecraft silently hovering above the desert floor before vanishing into thin air. And let's not forget the occasional report of a good old-fashioned abduction—because what's a UFO hotspot without a little alien kidnapping?

But what makes Hooper such a prime spot for close encounters of the third kind? Experts (and by "experts," I mean people who spend a lot of time looking up at the night sky) have their theories. One camp believes that the area's geothermal activity—hot springs, underground rivers, and the like—attracts UFOs. The theory is that extraterrestrials are drawn to the Earth's natural power sources like moths to a flame. After all, why travel across the universe just to abduct some guy from a cornfield when you can check out Earth's geothermal wonders instead?

The opposing camp, let's call them the skeptics, insists there's a more logical explanation. According to them, the isolation of the valley, combined with the intense, pitch-black darkness that falls over the landscape at night, plays tricks on the mind. It's not UFOs, they say—it's just your imagination, and maybe a stray satellite or two. The San Luis Valley, after all, is so far removed from city lights that even the faintest light in the sky can look like an alien spacecraft coming to probe your cows.

So, who's right? Is Hooper really a cosmic rest stop for alien travelers, or are people just seeing things that aren't there? Well, as with most things UFO-related, the truth is probably somewhere out there, hovering in a gray area (pun fully intended). But that hasn't stopped the Watchtower from becoming a pilgrimage site for UFO enthusiasts and the merely curious alike.

For those who do make the journey to Hooper, there's more to the UFO Watchtower than just, well, watching the sky. Surrounding the tower is a bizarre, eclectic collection of offerings left behind by visitors—everything from old shoes to car keys to handwritten notes asking the aliens for luck, love, or just a safe trip home. Locals say these objects are part of the "cosmic vortex" that supposedly exists in the area. You know, the usual New Age stuff—energy fields, spiritual connections, and maybe, just maybe, a portal to another dimension. No big deal.

If you ask the locals, though, the real charm of the Watchtower isn't just the hope of seeing a UFO—it's the sense of community that's formed around it. Whether you're a true believer or just passing through, there's something strangely comforting about standing on that metal platform, staring up at the stars with a bunch of strangers, all sharing the same hope: that tonight might be the night you finally catch a glimpse of the unknown.

Of course, even if you don't spot a flying saucer, there's always the chance you'll meet someone who swears they did. And in a place like Hooper, that's almost as good. After all, where else can you get a firsthand account of an alien sighting from a guy wearing a tinfoil hat while munching on a burrito from the nearby taco stand?

So, the next time you find yourself in southern Colorado, take a detour to the UFO Watchtower in Hooper. Whether you leave a believer or not, one thing's for sure: you'll have a story to tell. And maybe, just maybe, you'll be the one to finally prove that we're not alone in the universe—or at least in the San Luis Valley.

Denver Airport Conspiracy Fears

Ah, Denver International Airport (DIA), the gateway to the Rockies. It's a sprawling, behemoth of an airport where your layovers feel longer than your flights, and getting from one gate to another involves the kind of planning that would make a military strategist sweat. But there's something else about DIA that sets it apart from your average airport. No, it's not just the size or the fancy automated trains whisking travelers from terminal to terminal—it's the fact that DIA might just be one of the most conspiracy-laden airports in the world.

You see, there are stories about DIA. A lot of stories. It's as if the place was custom-built for the tinfoil-hat crowd. What started as a few whispers back in the 90s has now ballooned into a full-blown avalanche of theories. Whether it's secret underground bunkers, hidden messages, or apocalyptic art, people are convinced there's more to Denver International Airport than meets the eye. And you know what? They're not wrong. Just maybe not in the way they think.

Let's start at the beginning. DIA opened in 1995, and it was 16 months late and about $2 billion over budget. (Cue dramatic music.) It's also massive—like *ridiculously* massive.

At over 33,000 acres, it's the largest airport in the United States. To give you some perspective, it's almost twice the size of the next largest airport. It's so big that if you didn't know better, you'd think it was secretly a small city—or, according to some, the headquarters for a future global takeover. You know, casual stuff.

That's where the theories start to take off, much like the planes it houses. Some people believe the construction delays and ballooning costs were due to the fact that DIA wasn't just an airport—it was a cover-up for something else. A former construction worker even claimed there are five underground buildings beneath the airport, and no one's quite sure what they're for. A top-secret government bunker, perhaps? Maybe an alien base? Or the world's weirdest subterranean shopping mall? The possibilities are endless!

Of course, no great conspiracy would be complete without a touch of the occult, and DIA delivers. Literally. There's a dedication stone in the airport that's adorned with—wait for it—a Masonic symbol. (Dun dun dunnn!) Oh, but it gets better. The stone also gives a shout-out to something called the "New World Airport Commission," a name that has launched a thousand theories. To be clear, this commission doesn't seem to exist anywhere outside of that stone. Conspiracy theorists took one look at that and said, "New World *Order*, anyone?" And who can blame them? With a name like that, it's like they were *asking* for it.

But we haven't even gotten to the murals yet. Oh, the murals. If you've been to DIA, you've probably noticed the giant, colorful wall paintings that look like something out of a dystopian fever dream. People point to these murals as proof that DIA is, in fact, a front for some apocalyptic New World Order plot. One mural in particular depicts soldiers in gas masks, children mourning dead animals, and—because this wouldn't be complete without a touch of menace—people huddled in what looks like a post-apocalyptic wasteland. It's like if Picasso and Orwell teamed up for a little lighthearted decor.

Of course, DIA insists the murals are meant to promote world peace and unity. But let's be real—nothing says "world peace" quite like a guy in a gas mask brandishing a sword. Right?

And let's not forget the pièce de résistance—the one conspiracy that truly defines DIA: Blucifer. If you haven't met Blucifer, let me introduce you. He's a giant, 32-foot-tall blue horse statue with glowing red eyes that stands guard outside the airport. Officially named "Blue Mustang," but lovingly dubbed Blucifer by locals, this demonic-looking creature has become DIA's unofficial mascot. Fun fact: the statue actually killed its creator, artist Luis Jiménez, when a piece of it fell on him during its construction. The statue literally has a body count. And people wonder why it's the stuff of nightmares.

Theories about Blucifer range from him being a symbol of the impending apocalypse to a harbinger of death. Or, you know, maybe he's just a really weird piece of modern art that's there to keep you awake after a long flight. Either way, you can't ignore him. He's practically daring you to make eye contact.

So, is there really something sinister going on at Denver International Airport? Honestly, probably not. The airport's officials have addressed the rumors multiple times, often with tongue planted firmly in cheek. In fact, they've even leaned into the conspiracy culture, putting up posters and artwork that jokingly refer to the wild stories. It's like they're saying, "Yes, we *could* be hiding something... but you'll never know for sure."

In the end, DIA's conspiracies are probably nothing more than a combination of coincidence, weird art choices, and good old-fashioned overactive imaginations. But that doesn't mean it isn't fun to speculate. And let's face it—whether or not there's a secret underground bunker beneath the airport, it's still a lot more interesting than waiting for your flight at Gate C34.

So next time you're stuck at DIA, take a moment to look around. Maybe you'll catch a glimpse of Blucifer's red eyes glaring at you through the terminal windows, or maybe you'll hear the faint knock of construction workers hammering away at a mysterious underground bunker. Whatever you do, just don't let the New World Order catch you snooping around. After all, they've got flights to run.

Beneath Cheyenne Mountain: A Secret World

On the surface, Cheyenne Mountain looks like your typical, majestic Rocky Mountain peak—looming tall and rugged, just outside Colorado Springs. Hikers and locals probably admire it every day, unaware that deep inside that picturesque mountain is one of the most secure and secretive military installations in the world. That's right, folks, Cheyenne Mountain is not just a scenic backdrop for your Instagram shots. It's a literal mountain fortress, and not just any fortress—a nuclear bunker with specs so wild they sound like something straight out of a Bond villain's playbook.

Welcome to the Cheyenne Mountain Complex. Or, as it's affectionately known in military circles: "The Hole." Now, I know what you're thinking. Who hides a military base inside a mountain? Well, apparently, the U.S. government does. It's the kind of thing you'd expect to see in a sci-fi movie, but nope, it's real, and it's been there since the Cold War. Back in the day, when the world was one misstep away from nuclear catastrophe, the powers-that-be figured the best way to keep an eye on the skies and protect the country from Armageddon was to put a control center where nothing short of a direct meteor strike could reach it—inside 2,000 feet of solid granite.

Now, granite, as it turns out, is a pretty handy thing when you're trying to build a place that can withstand *literally* anything. They designed the Cheyenne Mountain Complex to take a 30 megaton nuclear blast from just a mile away, which, if you're wondering, is enough force to obliterate just about anything *except* this mountain. Just in case you aren't up-to-date on your nuclear lingo, a 30 megaton explosion is twice as powerful as the largest bomb the U.S. ever tested, and for perspective, it's over 1,500 times stronger than the bomb that destroyed Hiroshima. So yeah, they weren't kidding around.

But let's not gloss over the doors, because no secret bunker worth its salt would be complete without some absurdly massive doors, right? The ones here are 25 tons each. That's about the weight of four African elephants, per door, give or take a tusk. When they shut, it's like slamming the vault door on a massive underground bank of national security. Only instead of gold, they're protecting... well, probably a lot of classified stuff that we can't talk about. And maybe a vending machine or two.

So what's this impenetrable fortress inside the belly of a mountain for, you ask? Back in the good ol' days, it was the nerve center for NORAD (North American Aerospace

Defense Command) and the U.S. Space Command. Its primary job was monitoring the airspace above North America for anything suspicious—missiles, enemy planes, UFOs... you know, the usual Cold War threats. There's something comforting (and slightly terrifying) about knowing that, tucked inside a mountain, there were military officers ready to scramble the jets at a moment's notice because someone picked up a blip on the radar. It's like the world's most intense game of Pong, but the stakes were nuclear.

Fast forward to today, and the Cheyenne Mountain Complex is still around, though its role has evolved. It's no longer the nerve center for NORAD (that job has moved down the road to Peterson Space Force Base). As of 2008, Cheyenne Mountain is now more of a backup operations center, used for things like flight crew training, monitoring data, and—oh yeah—still serving as a fully operational bunker in case things go sideways. It's basically a giant insurance policy, in granite form.

But let's not get too carried away with all the serious talk—because you know, there's something kind of absurd about it all. For instance, despite being a highly secretive and secure military base, Cheyenne Mountain Complex is probably the most famous "secret" anyone in Colorado has ever heard of. It's been featured in more TV shows and movies than you can count. If you've watched *Stargate SG-1*, *WarGames*, or pretty much any Hollywood film that needed a high-tech military base hidden in a mountain, then congratulations—you've seen Cheyenne Mountain in all its fictionalized glory.

Hollywood makes it look like the place is filled with laser gates, robots, and alien portals, but reality is a little less flashy. Sure, there are the 25-ton blast doors, the network of tunnels, and all the high-tech equipment you'd expect in a place designed to survive nuclear fallout, but sadly, no alien technology or time travel devices—at least not that we know of. Let's be honest, if they did have a Stargate, it would probably still be classified.

And if you think the only thing wild about this place is its infrastructure, think again. The mountain itself is pretty intense. Cheyenne Mountain is sitting on a seismic buffer, so even if the ground starts shaking (because let's face it, if you've survived nuclear apocalypse, what's an earthquake?), this place isn't going anywhere. It's like building a skyscraper on top of a bouncy castle—except in this case, the bouncy castle is designed to keep the apocalypse out.

In the end, Cheyenne Mountain Complex isn't just a relic of Cold War paranoia—it's a testament to humanity's creativity when faced with existential threats. I mean, who looks at a giant mountain and thinks, "Yeah, let's turn that into a high-tech fortress?" The same people who built the Internet, that's who. The same people who decided that sending a lightning bolt through the entire town of Colorado Springs (looking at you, Tesla) was a good idea. Colorado has always been a state for big ideas, and the idea of hiding an entire military base inside a mountain has to rank up there with the wildest of them all.

So, next time you're admiring the scenic beauty of Cheyenne Mountain on your drive through Colorado Springs, just remember—you're looking at more than just a pretty peak. Inside that mountain, the legacy of Cold War intrigue and military might lives on. And maybe, just maybe, someone's in there right now, flipping through the channels and watching *Stargate* for the hundredth time, chuckling at how close (or far off) Hollywood really got it.

The Lost Graves of Cheesman Park

Picture this: you're enjoying a sunny day at Cheesman Park in Denver. The birds are singing, kids are playing, and the majestic Rocky Mountains loom in the distance. It's a perfect spot for a picnic, a jog, or a lazy afternoon of cloud-watching. What you might not know is that, just beneath the carefully manicured lawns and picturesque scenery, there's a chilling secret: you're probably sitting on someone's unmarked grave.

Cheesman Park, you see, wasn't always the idyllic urban oasis it is today. In fact, in the late 1800s, it was a massive cemetery—a final resting place for the pioneers, the criminals, and just about anyone in between who shuffled off this mortal coil in early Denver. Originally a 320-acre plot perched on the outskirts of town, Mount Prospect Cemetery, as it was once called, was a peaceful spot for the dead. That is, until the living started moving in.

As Denver grew, it turned out that prime real estate near the heart of the city was just too valuable to be wasted on, well... corpses. By the 1890s, the cemetery was in bad shape—headstones were crumbling, weeds ran wild, and some of the graves hadn't been touched in years. The once-serene burial ground had become an eyesore. The solution? Evict the dead and turn the space into a park for the living. Simple, right? Oh, if only.

The process of moving the graves began in 1890, and that's when things got... messy. You see, the wealthier residents of the cemetery, whose families could afford nice tombstones and memorials, were pretty easy to locate and move. Their remains were carefully transferred to other cemeteries around town. But the poor, the unclaimed, and the criminals buried in the less glamorous sections? Not so much.

Enter E.P. McGovern, the man hired by the city to handle the removal of thousands of bodies. Paid per casket, McGovern quickly figured out a way to make this job as profitable as possible—by cutting corners, literally. Instead of respectfully relocating each full set of remains, McGovern and his team started chopping up the bodies and stuffing them into child-sized coffins. Smaller caskets meant more caskets, which meant more money. It was a grotesque assembly line of dismemberment, all in the name of profit.

If you're imagining a dignified exhumation process, think again. Workers were hacking apart skeletons, filling up multiple coffins with body parts from different people, and, in some cases, just leaving body parts behind entirely. Unsurprisingly, the whole operation caused quite a scandal. Imagine looking out your window in 1893 and seeing your local graveyard transformed into a horror show of exposed bones, empty coffins, and open graves. It wasn't long before the public outcry became too loud to ignore. The city, realizing things had gone off the rails, fired McGovern and halted the exhumation process. But by then, the damage had been done.

So what did the city do next? Well, rather than finish the job, they did what any good urban planner might: they covered it up. Literally. They smoothed over the land, planted some trees, and eventually turned the area into Cheesman Park, the Denver Botanical Gardens, and City Park. Voila! Problem solved—out of sight, out of mind. Except, of course, for the thousands of bodies that never got moved.

To this day, beneath the grass and jogging paths of Cheesman Park, the forgotten dead remain. Historians estimate that as many as 2,000 bodies are still buried under the park, a ghostly reminder of Denver's less-than-dignified handling of its early cemetery. And as if that wasn't eerie enough, there are still occasional reports of bones surfacing. Imagine walking your dog and stumbling upon a human femur. Not quite the peaceful afternoon you had in mind, right?

And then there are the ghost stories. Some say that on the brightest of full-moon nights, you can still see the outlines of where the old graves once were, their presence marked by patches of grass that seem just a little bit darker than the rest. Others claim to have heard strange whispers in the park at night, or seen ghostly figures wandering the grounds.

The souls of Denver's forgotten dead, perhaps, making their displeasure known.

It's the kind of story that makes you wonder—next time you're lounging on a picnic blanket in Cheesman Park, enjoying a sandwich and soaking up the sun, are you really alone? Or are you sharing your lunch with a few hundred restless spirits, buried just a few feet beneath you?

Hey, it gives new meaning to "dining with the dead," doesn't it?

So, while Cheesman Park is one of Denver's most beloved green spaces today, it's worth remembering that the park's history is just a *little* darker than the average city playground. From mass graves to scandalous gravediggers, the tale of Denver's lost cemetery is a reminder that sometimes, the past is literally buried beneath our feet. Just hope it stays there.

Tales of Alma

Nestled high in the Rocky Mountains at an elevation of 10,578 feet, Alma, Colorado, is often referred to as the highest incorporated town in North America. Founded during the gold rush of the 1860s, Alma has weathered its share of highs and lows, both in terms of the economy and the legends that have taken root in its picturesque setting. The town's historic buildings, ghost stories, and folklore weave a rich tapestry that tells the story of a once-bustling mining camp turned quiet community.

From its beginnings as a vibrant mining hub to its current status as a quaint getaway, Alma's tales echo through the pines and whisper through the winds. The stories of the town's inhabitants, both living and departed, have shaped the identity of Alma, drawing visitors eager to explore its past.

The lore of Alma began in the wake of the Colorado Gold Rush when prospectors flooded into the region, drawn by the promise of fortune and adventure. Established in 1860, Alma was originally known as "Boreas" until it was renamed after a nearby creek. At its peak, the town boasted hotels, saloons, and general stores, thriving on the gold mined from the surrounding hills.

Among the most notable characters of this era was David H. McGowan, an influential figure in Alma's early days.

McGowan was not just a miner; he was a businessman who saw the potential of the town and helped shape its development. His story is intertwined with tales of ambition and misfortune, embodying the spirit of those who came seeking their dreams in the mountains.

As miners flocked to Alma, the town became known for its colorful characters. Prospectors, gamblers, and dreamers mingled in the local saloons, where the atmosphere was charged with excitement and possibility. However, with opportunity came peril; many met untimely ends in the rugged wilderness or succumbed to the dangers of mining. These lost souls are said to haunt the town to this day, contributing to Alma's ghostly reputation.

The spirit of Alma is palpably present in its ghost stories, many of which revolve around the former hotels and saloons that once buzzed with life. The Alma Hotel, built in the late 1800s, is a prime location for ghostly encounters. Visitors and staff have reported sightings of a spectral figure believed to be that of a former owner, who appears in the hallways and rooms. Some claim she tends to the guests as if ensuring their comfort, while others have felt an icy chill pass through the building.

Another infamous site is the Boreas Pass, a historic railroad pass that once served as a crucial route for transporting goods and people. Legends say that the spirits of those who lost their lives on the treacherous tracks still roam the area, sometimes manifesting as mysterious lights or unexplained sounds echoing through the mountains. The old train tracks, now abandoned and overgrown, serve as a reminder of the lives entwined with the land, leaving an eerie yet fascinating legacy.

One particularly captivating tale involves a miner who was said to have hidden his gold in a secret location before succumbing to a tragic accident. Locals believe that his spirit remains in Alma, guarding his treasure, and many have attempted to uncover his hidden fortune, only to be thwarted by the miner's spectral presence. Whether they were chasing shadows or truly encountering the ghost of the legendary miner, the excitement of the hunt lingers on in Alma's lore.

The rugged beauty of Alma's landscape plays a significant role in shaping its stories. The snow-capped peaks and dense forests provide an atmospheric backdrop, amplifying the sense of mystery and wonder. Many believe that nature itself is infused with the spirits of those who have come and gone, contributing to a unique energy that pervades the town.

In winter, Alma transforms into a quiet haven, blanketed in snow and solitude. Visitors often report feeling a deep connection to the past during this season, as the stark beauty evokes reflections on the struggles and triumphs of those who once walked the same paths. Ghostly figures are said to flit through the snow-covered trees, whispering tales of old and beckoning the curious to listen closely.

Moreover, the nearby South Park area, rich in both history and folklore, adds to the legends of Alma. The region is known for its mythical creatures, including Bigfoot, with many enthusiasts venturing into the wild in search of evidence. Stories of strange sounds and fleeting glimpses of creatures in the shadows

Today, Alma is a small community with a population that hovers around 250, yet its legends continue to attract visitors year-round. The blend of history, natural beauty, and the supernatural creates a unique charm that captivates adventurers, history buffs, and ghost hunters alike. The annual Alma's Arts and Music Festival draws crowds eager to celebrate the town's heritage while keeping its stories alive.

Alma's legacy is also preserved in its historic buildings, which are lovingly maintained by locals. Walking through the town feels like stepping back in time, where every creak of the floorboards and flickering of the old gas lamps hints at the lives once lived there. Guided ghost tours have become popular, allowing guests to delve into the town's haunted history while sharing a laugh at the quirks of its past.

In essence, the tales of Alma are not just stories; they are threads in the fabric of the town's identity. They remind us of the dreams and struggles of those who came before us, making Alma a living testament to the enduring spirit of the

American West. As the sun sets behind the mountains, casting a golden glow over the quaint buildings, one can't help but feel that the ghosts of Alma still walk among us, sharing their stories, and reminding us to listen to the echoes of the past.

With its unique combination of history and ghostly tales, Alma continues to intrigue and inspire those who wander through its storied streets, ensuring that its legends live on for generations to come.

The Journey Continues... With You.

As we reach the end of this exploration into the myths and legends of Colorado, I want to take a moment to express my heartfelt gratitude to you, the reader. Thank you for embarking on this journey with me—one that weaves together the threads of history, folklore, and the captivating tales that have shaped the cultural landscape of this remarkable state.

From the haunting whispers of Silver Heels wandering through the ghost towns to the brave stories of pioneers and the enigmatic creatures lurking in the shadows of the Rockies, we've uncovered a tapestry rich with the essence of Colorado. Each tale we've explored has been a window into the past, inviting us to consider how the stories we share shape our understanding of who we are today.

As we traversed the pages, we encountered the enduring legends of Native American cultures, whose rich traditions continue to resonate with the land. The stories of the Ute, Cheyenne, and Arapaho peoples remind us that Colorado's history is as diverse as its stunning landscapes. We've delved into the fascinating myths surrounding lost treasures, ghostly apparitions, and daring escapades that echo through time. With each legend, we peeled back layers of mystery and intrigue, illuminating the connections between the past and the present.

But remember, the journey does not end here! I encourage you to step outside the pages of this book and into the vibrant landscapes that inspired these legends. Whether it's hiking the trails of Mount Evans, wandering through the quaint streets of Breckenridge, or standing beneath the towering peaks of the San Juan Mountains, each experience offers its own sense of adventure and discovery. Seek out the historic sites, engage with local storytellers, and listen for the echoes of the past in the rustle of the trees or the rush of a mountain stream. The myths and legends of Colorado are not just stories confined to history; they are living narratives waiting to be experienced firsthand.

Consider planning a weekend getaway to one of Colorado's many ghost towns, where the echoes of the past still linger among the crumbling buildings and rusting machinery. Explore the winding paths of Cripple Creek, where the spirits of miners and dreamers once roamed, or visit the eerie remnants of St. Elmo, where the past feels remarkably present. With every step, you'll find that the stories you read here come alive in ways that are both exhilarating and poignant.

If you are lucky enough to encounter locals or fellow travelers, I encourage you to share your newfound knowledge and enthusiasm for the legends that weave through Colorado's history. Perhaps you'll hear a story you haven't yet discovered or learn about a hidden gem waiting to be explored. The beauty of these myths is that they often change shape and form with each telling, enriched by the experiences and perspectives of those who share them.

And if you found joy, inspiration, or even a sense of wonder within these pages, I kindly ask you to share that experience with others. Leaving a review at your favorite online book retailer is a small yet meaningful way to help fellow readers discover the myths and legends that make Colorado such a special place. Your insights and reflections can illuminate the path for others who are eager to explore the captivating history and folklore of this magnificent state.

In addition to sharing your thoughts through a review, consider discussing the legends you've encountered with friends and family. Share a tale around the campfire or during a leisurely evening at home. It's a wonderful way to keep these stories alive, fostering a sense of community and connection through the shared experience of storytelling. Who knows? You might inspire someone else to embark on their own adventure of exploration!

As we reflect on the tales we've shared, it's essential to recognize the importance of preserving these legends for future generations. The stories that have shaped our understanding of Colorado's past are also a vital part of our cultural heritage. By engaging with these myths and legends, we contribute to a collective memory that honors the experiences of those who came before us. Encourage others to explore and appreciate the unique folklore of their own communities as well.

In closing, I hope this book has sparked your curiosity and encouraged you to embrace the stories that surround you. As you venture forth into the beautiful landscapes of Colorado, carry these legends with you and remember that the spirit of adventure lies in every corner, waiting for those who dare to seek it out.

Thank you once again for joining me on this journey. May your own adventures be filled with the magic of Colorado's myths and the thrill of discovery. Remember, every mountain has its tale, every river its secret, and every shadow its spirit. Happy exploring!

If you've enjoyed this book

Please consider leaving a review at your favorite online book retailer. Think of it as sending a cookie to the author without the calories or the awkward "I made these from scratch" small talk. Plus, it helps other readers find this gem—or at least something shiny enough to distract them while they're looking for the next great adventure!